Punishment
on
Trial

Punishment
on
Trial

Ennio Cipani
Alliant International University

CONTEXT PRESS
Reno, Nevada

Punishment on Trial

Paperback pp. 137

Library of Congress Cataloging-in-Publication Data

Cipani, Ennio.
  Punishment on trial / Ennio Cipani.
    p. cm.
  Includes bibliographical references.
    ISBN 1-878978-51-9 (pbk.)
  1. Discipline of children. 2. Behavior modification. I. Title.
    HQ770.4.C46 2004
    649'.64–dc22

                                        2004018062

                                    © 2004 CONTEXT PRESS
                          933 Gear Street, Reno, NV 89503-2729

Printed in the United States of America

Cover design by Vanessa Cipani.

Dedication

This book serves as a memorial to my late mother, Elvira Portante Cipani, who granted me lessons about life that cannot be found in any classes.

About the Author

Ennio Cipani received his Ph.D. in educational psychology from Florida State University in 1979. He has been a licensed psychologist is California since 1983, and is the director of Cipani & Associates, a behavioral and educational consulting company. In this capacity he and his behavioral specialists have served many families, providing in-home behavioral parent teaching/training services. He and his wife, Lucinda, also have three children of their own: Lorenzo, Vanessa, and Alessandra.

He is currently a professor in clinical psychology at Alliant International University and has previously taught at the University of the Pacific in the Department of Special Education. He has published numerous books, professional articles, and behavior management materials for parents and teachers. For more complete information about the author, go to his web site at *www.geocities.com/voivod00* (2 zeros at the end).

Preface

Do you:

- Equate spanking with punishment?
- Ground your teenager, to no avail?
- Believe punishment does not work for your child?
- Believe punishment does not teach the child appropriate behavior?
- Make common mistakes in using time-out?
- Hear from professionals that punishing children for misbehavior is abusive, and doesn't even work?
- Feel guilty when you sense that you should punish your child for some misbehavior, but have been told that such is bad parenting?

If you answered, "Yes" to one or more of the above questions, this book may be just the definitive resource you have been waiting for. Punishment is a controversial topic, but one that parents face daily: to use or not to use? I have worked with many parents who are haunted by ill feelings when they resort to consequences for their children's misbehavior. They are told punishment is often ineffective. They have been led to believe that their actions have more to do with their own needs than a desire to teach their children right from wrong. In some cases, they are made to feel that they may have possibly facilitated negative long-term effects on their children's development, or even engaged in abusive behavior. Many parents therefore question the use of punishment, but have not come up with an effective alternative. As a result, they use it sporadically and hence render it ineffective.

Professionals, parents and teachers need answers that are based on factual information. *Punishment on Trial* provides that source. Effective punishment can take many forms, most of which do not involve physical punishment. This book demystifies punishment for the reader. *Punishment on Trial* explores common myths held about punishment, and presents scientific evidence and logic to debunk such myths. Techniques that alter undesirable child behavior, backed by research studies a well as real live cases, are presented. Finally a model for a responsible use of punishment is presented.

I have attempted to convey this information in an easy to read and entertaining style, while providing a factual basis for the information. This book hopefully presents a nice blend of science, clinical experience, and logic to a discussion of the efficacy of punishment for child behavior problems.

Acknowledgements

I am indebted to Dr. Mary Burch, Petra Sutton and Lucy DeRose for their constructive editing of the manuscript. I would also like to express my appreciation to Steve Eversol, Hiroaki Uemura, Adam Nelson, and Gloria Lopez for their thoughtful comments on earlier drafts of the book. I also thank Vanessa Cipani for her design of the book cover. Finally, I wish to thank Dr. Jon Bailey, Florida State University, for all of his help and advice over the past 27 years.

Table of Contents

x

Cases

Introduction

Punishment as a means to change misbehavior of children is a controversial topic, to say the least. Persons advocating the use of punishment and those people who are against the use of punishment have often resorted to claims that may or may not have a basis in scientific evidence. What is even more distressing is that the validity of such claims and theories is rarely questioned or judged. Uttering the words, "We have research that shows," or "We have findings," often is taken to sanctify whatever position is being proposed, without any independent judgment of the validity of the purported research. Therefore the claims made on the basis of such research often go unquestioned.

How controversial is this topic? If you advocate for the use of punishment, your professional and personal reputation is questioned and your expertise is debased. Many people in professional and administrative capacities have had to quickly refute their position on punishment, to avoid severe professional and political consequences. Galileo's dealings with the papacy in the 16th century may seem like small claims court when compared to the wrath of people who stand to judge those who support the use of punishment. Further, what is considered off limits, in both practice and research inquires from the professional police squad, can be a most innocuous consequence for child behavior (to most American parents).

Lest I give you the impression that the zealots just exist on the side demanding that any form of punishment be outlawed, let me correct that impression. The advocates for using physical punishment can be just as adamant. There is a rising tide in this country that attributes much of our woes in raising children (or our inability to do such) to the removal of corporal punishment in schools and homes.

The topic of punishment is rarely portrayed as a useful strategy in books and professional presentations. Many authors skirt the topic, for fear of retribution by either side. On the one hand you have some people intimating that you are an abusive adult if you state that your child has broken a rule, in a voice harsher than Mr. Rogers. If you then proceed to "punish" the child by making him miss cartoons that afternoon for the infraction, you have really stepped over the line. According to these experts, you may even have gone so far as to destroy his self-esteem and produce long-term damage to his psychological disposition when he enters adulthood! These people equate punishment with abusive behavior. They rely on unproven theories to justify their vilification of punishment and the people that use it. They often cite cases in the media of child abuse, and equate such abuse with punishment, therefore, evidence that all punishment should be banned. The inference they want you to draw is the following. If a parent starts using punishment techniques, she or he is "on the road" to becoming a child abuser.

On the other extreme, some people believe that severe physical punishment is needed. Anything less is soft and un-American. Their evidence that punishment is lacking in today's society comes from the rash of school shootings, teenage pregnancies and other ills that would not be existent if corporal punishment were in full force. After all, spanking was a part of Americana when we were growing up. Look how much has changed for the worse.

I undertook the writing of this book to provide a basis of fact for adults struggling to make sense of their own discipline policies. Through a better understanding of the effects of punishment, and the conditions under which it is ineffective, parents and professionals would be better equipped to handle child behavior. A decision to use or not use punishment should be made on the scientific merits of a procedure. At the heart of the decision should be the goal of changing the behavior of children in the most effective and reasonable manner. Shouldn't your judgment about punishment be a function of how you want your child to behave and what is the best means of obtaining such behavior?

It is to this end that this book attempts to provide factual information and dispel some of the fictional representations regarding punishment. It does so by putting *punishment on trial*. I will provide research evidence on the efficacy of punishment procedures. Additionally, I will submit my own judgments, based on two decades of practice in child behavior therapy. It is of course your choice as to whether your own discipline strategy will incorporate certain consequences that might function as punishers. You, the reader will certainly be better informed regarding the truth about punishment (and also reinforcement). Hopefully this will allow you to place into a scientific perspective what you hear other people say about punishment.

This book will probably change your understanding of what constitutes punishment (in the technical sense). As your first test on what constitutes punishment, please read the case presented below. Was punishment used to deal with aggressive behavior on the playground?

The Case of Boys Will Be Boys—
Reducing Aggressive Behavior in Preschool Children

I was asked to consult with Head Start programs in regards to the behavioral problems of some of the children attending the morning or afternoon program. A prototype of a frequent request for consultation was for a child (usually a boy) who was aggressive to other children.

One of my first consultations was for a boy who was frequently aggressive. In my observation, I noted a phenomenon that seemed to be the catalyst for this child's aggression during the outside free play period. When the children were sent outside for playground activities, arguments and fights erupted around the use of the 3 available tricycles. As you might guess, about 10 kids wanted to ride the 3 bikes, all at the same time. The children argued and pushed each other away from the bike in order to establish themselves as the bike riders. Once a child landed in the seat, she or he usually went unchallenged (kind of like "King of the Mountain"). As you could guess, my client was quite good at getting the bike, and keeping it.

From my observation, I noted that the teachers did not seem to intervene during the squabbling over the bikes. I saw a child approach a teacher and complain, "Billy won't share the bike. He keeps riding it." The teacher bent down and said, 'Now Suzy, you go back to Billy and see if you can work something out." Suzy went back to Billy and apparently what got worked out was the following: If Suzy leaves Billy alone, he will not hit her or push her down. If she tries to take the bike from him, she will be judged as an intruder and dealt with."

I asked the teacher what her advice was over the dispute with the bike. She remarked, "Our philosophy here is that we want the children to learn to work out their problems on their own. If we solve their interpersonal squabbles and problems, they will never learn to develop self-control and personal responsibility to themselves and their fellow human being!" Ok, I see. That explains the mortal combat approach to child interactions on the playground. Maybe I misread the sign on the front of the building. Instead of observing a Head Start program, I must have mistakenly entered a toddler boot camp for future hockey players.

I first had to convince the teachers that the survival of the fittest contests for possession of the 3 bikes was a large contributing factor to aggression on the playground. Subsequently, the plan I set up had two components. First, any incident of aggression resulted in the offending child going to a time-out area for 3 minutes. That child could not play with any of the playground equipment or toys at this time, but merely sat on the bench for the 3-minute period. Following the time-out, she or he returned to play with any toy not being used by another child. This basically removed the opportunity to ride the bike for that play period for offenders.

The second component of the intervention focused on teaching children that a negotiated settlement is in their best interests. For example, if 2 or more children wanted to ride a given bike, one or both would come to the teacher and present their dilemma. The bike time was divided evenly. The teacher praised the children for bringing their problem to her and then set the portable oven timer for two minutes. One child was assigned to ride it for that 2-minute period. Following the timer ringing, that child would get off the bike and the teacher directed the other student to the bike for his or her 2-minute period. In summary, aggressive behavior resulted in time-out and loss of the opportunity to ride the bike. Bringing the matter to the "teacher's court" for judgment, and not taking matters into one's own hands, resulted in a negotiated settlement.

As you might have guessed, aggressive behavior dropped dramatically with this intervention. It is also important to note that the teachers remarked that the children were now bringing their issues surrounding toys and bikes to them more often. It is interesting how time-out will teach children to find a more acceptable way to work out their impulsive behavior. What was also an interesting finding in this program was that many of the children who needed the bike right away learned one of two things: how to wait, or how to find something else interesting to play with that was not in as great a demand as the bikes. Isn't human nature funny that way?

Overview of *Punishment on Trial*

This material is divided into four sections. The first section is entitled, *What is Punishment?* This section covers basic material with respect to "outcome-oriented punishment" as a means to change child behavior. The importance of using an outcome-oriented definition of punishment is stressed and the ramifications of such a definition are delineated. The second section, *Exposing Myths about Punishment,* reviews 5 misunderstandings surrounding punishment. The evidence regarding the myth (or lack thereof) is given and its validity debunked. Research supporting more valid conclusions is provided and the factors parents should consider are also provided.

In the third section, *Six Basic Principles,* requisite practices derived from scientific research on punishment are delineated. Such principles are often abused, violated and ignored, which leads to many misconceptions about punishment from lay and professional audiences alike. Throughout the book, personal clinical cases are detailed to illustrate a point. Subsequent to the case presentation, several questions are presented for you to contemplate. The last section, *A Responsible Use of Punishment,* covers the considerations when using punishment to change child behavior. If you choose to use consequences, this section will provide guidelines for implementation of a child behavior plan.

A Psychologist Who Makes House Calls

In this book, I present scientific evidence regarding the efficacy of punishment procedures as well as drawbacks. However, in certain areas, the research data are not overwhelming and/or compelling. I fill in these areas with actual cases of families in need of help, as well as my opinions based on serving many families over a two-decade period. However, you will be made aware of what is scientific fact and what represents conjecture on my part. To judge my opinions as credible (or not), I believe it is important to gain a perspective about my experience.

I came to California in 1981 in order to take a position at a university teacher-training program. Additionally, I was interested in clinical work and began contracting with agencies serving families who have children with developmental disabilities. While I had considerable experience working with this population in state institutions, this was my first experience working with families in their homes. A unique model of service called behavioral intervention service (BIS) was used. BIS was unlike anything I had seen before in its approach to providing help to families. BIS was a system that required me, as the professional, to go to the family's residence or the child's school and conduct the assessment of problem child behavior in the real life setting. In other words, it is an in-home, parent training, program. Even today this is unique within mental health programs, since services to clients are almost exclusively done in the professional office.

I would draw up a plan to deal with the child's problem behavior, by re-arranging the manner in which the parent(s) would deal with problem and appropriate behavior. Subsequent to the written plan, I initiated the parent training phase. Once again, this phase was conducted in the child's home, day care or school. Imagine that, a psychologist who makes house calls.

Being on the "battleground" served to educate me in a manner that very few other mental health professionals experience. Maybe in the treatment of physical illness, physicians do not have to see the person sick in their own home to appreciate the problem and the potential solution. After all, the target symptoms of the disease are probably as readily observable in the doctor's office as they would be in the child's home. However, the same is not the case with human behavior. How can one determine what really goes on when the family leaves the office? Unlike some helping professionals who may doubt the complaints of the parents as more a symptom of their pathology, I saw with my own eyes what transpired when it was time to come to the dinner table. You know the old saying, seeing is believing! And it truly can be an eye opening experience. My advice to people who want to help parents: See what it is like to walk in their shoes by showing up at homework time. Only then will you truly appreciate what these parents go through, day in and day out.

An additional advantage of this in-home model of training is that it allowed me to provide on-the-spot coaching to the parent. This approach is much more effective than sitting in an office trying to explain how to do something. Here is a case in point. A child, who was 4 at the time, engaged in disruptive or destructive behavior regularly. As I visited with his mother, his sister and him, the first time, I was amazed at what I saw for the next hour or so. As I watched him, while gathering basic information from his mother, it seemed as if there was not a minute that elapsed without his doing something disruptive and/or destructive. He was either hitting his sister, dumping utensils on the floor, slamming the door on the way outside, or throwing things in the house. He was running around the house like a hurricane feeding off moist air. I got tired just watching him and I was sitting down (and a lot younger than I am now).

I decided that it would be best if we targeted just one problem initially and let the others go for the time being. His mother did not seem to mind some of the "hyperactive" problems, so I felt that the aggression to his sister must be our first intervention target. I recommended that we use time-out to the corner when he hit or slapped his sister. She agreed and I demonstrated the time-out procedure to her before scheduling the next appointment. On the next home visit, she and I would deploy the time-out for acts of aggression toward his sister.

Upon my arrival on "D-Day," I reminded her of the time-out consequence for aggression toward his sister. I would watch and coach her while she monitored his behavior and provide time-out when he hit or slapped his sister. I can tell you that if I had not been there, the time-out program would not have even gotten one toe off the ground. It took several aggressions on his part, with my running in to provide the time-out, before she realized that she would have to watch him a little bit closer. I could almost see her remark; "This time-out plan is tougher than it sounds."

She did improve. Towards the end of the first training session, she was catching about half of the incidences without my cueing (still inadequate). If I had just seen her in my office, she probably would have reported that she tried the time-out and it did not work. I would not have been privy to the fact that she failed to use it. Here is a news flash for Associated Press: Time-out only works if you use it consistently. Simply announcing to the child that you are now a time-out trained parent does not impress the child if you don't follow through. Imagine that!

My opinion about the effects of punishment is not based solely on what surveys report many parents say about punishment. My clinical experience is not comprised primarily of talking to people about their problems, commiserating with their plight and then simply explaining behavior from a theoretical perspective. I was given the assignment of helping a family overcome some moderate to severe behavioral challenges exhibited by one or more of their children. My task was to problem solve on how such debilitating behaviors can be ameliorated or eliminated, to allow such families to grow as a unit in greater harmony.

Each time my behavioral specialists and I solved a behavioral problem, we grew in our understanding of how to help future families. Our being in the thick of things has allowed us to discern those procedures that are effective from those procedures that sound great but do not often deliver. I hope my experience with real life families in their homes makes for enjoyable reading!

Section I:
What is Punishment?

Punishment is a not just a controversial topic, it is often misunderstood. It can mean apples to one group of people and bananas to another. Yet both groups would insist, in heated arguments, that they are talking about the same phenomenon. One group would describe apples, and their color, texture and shape. The other group would violently reject this supposition, saying that if one were not color blind, one could plainly see that this phenomenon is yellow in color, and describe a banana. In other words, each group would describe a different phenomenon, but use the same term to define it.

How does the analogy about apples and bananas apply to punishment? Take a look at the examples below which are statements with a reference to punishment.

"He really punished him by sending him to his room."
"The boxer gave the challenger some punishing blows to the midsection."
"The man's punishment for driving without a license was 6 months probation."
"The child was punished for grabbing the cereal off the shelf."

Which of the above are examples of punishment? It depends on your definition of punishment. There have certainly been numerous books and other writings on the topic of punishment. A cursory review of an online book distributor (www.barnesandnoble.com) found over 1,200 books listed under the subject heading of punishment. You would think that with all that material there would be agreement on the phenomenon described as punishment. The vast majority of these books deal with punishment from the judicial perspective. Punishment is often equated with the sentence a judge (or jury) hands down when a guilty verdict is given. It is the imposition of a harsh set of conditions, as a result of some offending behavior, which characterizes punishment in much of these writings.

This perspective of punishment exemplifies what I will term as the "procedural definition of punishment" (Grusec & Walters, 1977). This definition merely requires the existence of two temporally ordered events (referred to as a contingency). First, some law violation behavior occurs (perpetrator is caught and successfully prosecuted). Second, the consequence is the imposition of the sentence, which is deemed to be of an aversive nature to the individual.

The procedural definition best fits the common use of the term, punishment, when referring to examples of punishment. Punishment is viewed as the imposition of a harsh consequence for a child's misbehavior. There exists a conditional relationship between what the child does and a consequence that befalls him or her.

If the child engages in a misbehavior, then a harsh or aversive condition is imposed. This is how many people define punishment.

What are some examples of this procedural use of the term, punishment? If Johnny hits his sister, he will go to bed. If Suzie has a tantrum, she will be sent to the corner for 20 minutes. If Raul hits his mother, he will get spanked. According to the procedural definition, the existence of punishment is determined via a subjective judgment regarding the harshness of the consequence. Did Johnny, Suzy, and Raul all receive punishment? Well, that depends on you, the judge.

With regard to the first example, was punishment delivered to Johnny for hitting his sister? You might say "yes," but others may question whether being sent to bed for hitting one's sister really constitutes punishment. Their response might be along the following line: "Going to bed is a punishment for not eating your vegetables. It's not adequate for a child who hits his sister? You have to teach him a lesson. Something far worse should be done, like taking away TV time for a week. But only one night of punishment? This is not right."

As you can see, being sent to bed would not, in the eyes of some, constitute an appropriate consequence for hitting one's sister, particularly if the incident caused injury. Who is right? Just as beauty is in the eye of the beholder, so too is punishment when using a procedural definition. What is harsh to one person is mild to another.

Note that in the above examples, the effect on the child's behavior is not specified. I believe this to be a huge and common mistake in discussions of punishment and one that leads to the widespread misunderstanding of punishment. Why is it important to specify what the effect on behavior is? Let's use the third example above to illustrate the ambiguity one faces when using the procedural (but highly subjective) approach to defining punishment. When Raul hits his mother, he will get spanked. Raul engages in this undesirable behavior and the presumed harsh (aversive) consequence is applied, i.e., spanking. Let us imagine that this harsh consequence is not effective. In other words, Raul still hits his mother when he is mad at her for not letting him watch TV. What are we to conclude? Punishment does not work for Raul? As his mother might utter, "Raul is beyond that of normal mortals, he is unaffected by punishment." If a child is not fazed by punishment, what can possibly help? "Probably only some miracle behavior drug that has yet to be discovered," mutters Raul's mother.

The pitfall with the procedural definition is that it attempts to account for the success or failure of punishment on the basis of a given application. If some consequence, which appears to be so aversive that it should affect child behavior, does not work, punishment itself is determined to be ineffective.

Concluding that punishment, as a general method of discipline, does not work leads to other more disastrous fall out. When parents or adults conclude this, they often do one of two things. First, they may claim that punishment does not work for their particular child. If punishment does not work, what else can be done for their child? "No sense trying something else along the same lines," is the faulty reasoning here. The unfortunate by-product of this conclusion is giving up on the effort to change behavior via consequences. They justify this conclusion by explaining the existence of behavior in terms of an unalterable condition, a condition inherent in the child's biology. I have often heard the following as an explanation for the failure of a consequence to change behavior: "Well, you know Johnny is just Johnny. He does this because he is just being Johnny." Translation: Since punishment does not work, it is in Johnny's nature to do what he does and nothing is going to change that!

Alternatively, the adult may conclude that not enough punishment (meaning magnitude or amount) was administered. This can be potentially more dangerous in the hands of novices than simply giving up. Their solution is to alter the intensity or duration of the consequent event. If you were spanking him once for hitting you, maybe you should spank him twice, or thrice. Maybe you should pull his pants down so he will really feel it.

As you can readily see this is a slippery slope. Many an abusive situation was unintentionally rendered in the search for a really, really harsh consequence, to effect a change in behavior. In the 1970s some children and adults living in institutions were sent to time-out: for two to three days in a box, with minimal food and water. The thought there must have been, if 2 hour time-outs were ineffective, maybe three days will do the trick. Failing to understand what constitutes punishment and how it works, I believe, is in large part, responsible for such abusive practices.

Punishment is Outcome-oriented

Concluding nothing can work, or escalating consequences to unsafe levels, can be the downfall of a procedural definition. Such results are less likely when an "outcome-oriented definition" (Grusec & Walters, 1977) is used. In an outcome-oriented definition, a procedural contingency (i.e., temporal relationship between behavior and a consequence) is still existent. However, an additional requirement is that the effect of this contingency on the behavior is one of decrease. Punishment as a phenomenon exists when a procedural (behavioral) contingency produces a decrease in the level of the target behavior. If one is interested in decreasing a behavior, punishment always works!

With outcome-oriented punishment, there is no need to judge the harshness of the consequence. If Johnny gets sent to bed early when he hits his sister, and he stops hitting his sister as a function of that consequence, then punishment exists. One cannot judge the presence of punishment simply by examining the consequence. Rather one must know what behavioral effect resulted when such a contingency was put in place. This use of the term punishment leads to some interesting corollaries.

First, punishment does not necessarily equate with the most severe forms of consequences. Punishment can occur with a consequence that certainly does not evoke physical pain in the individual (as this book will make abundantly evident). One need not be concerned about a subjective appraisal of the intended consequence. Rather one should be concerned with the resultant effect. This definition stipulates an outcome-oriented requirement.

Second, to equate the term punishment, with spankings, paddling, or any other form of corporal punishment is incorrect. In the previous example, if spanking produces a decrease in Raul hitting his mother, then punishment occurred.

Spanking is a punisher in this situation. Spanking may not have the same effect with another child, or in another context. Further, one should not equate having a "tough" discipline practice with being effective. Mr. Felser, in the real life scenario depicted below, probably thought he practiced tough discipline when he paddled students in junior high for "breaking the silence." I can personally attest to his toughness. But was he effective?

What Really Happened in the "Good Ole Days?"

In 1965, I was in seventh grade in a brand new junior high school, in Lake Ronkonkoma, New York. The wrestling coach, who also was the industrial arts teacher, was in charge of the cafeteria during my lunch period. I would guess there were several hundred students who ate lunch at each shift. Prior to each lunch shift being dismissed to go back to classes, Mr. Felser (not his real name) would signal the students, via microphone, that "quiet time" had ensued. During quiet time, students were to sit quietly, put their tray up, and not utter a peep to their neighbor.

The consequence for being caught talking during quiet time were a function of one's previous number of infractions. The first time you were caught, Mr. Felser broadcast your infraction to everyone: "Mr. Sundin, please stand. You have just been awarded cleaning duty." You then were assigned to clean up the cafeteria. With your second incident, you received the above consequence as well as a scheduled spanking with a paddle (actually you could choose either a paddling or a detention). The third time you got all three.

When quiet time was signaled, the cafeteria became noticeably quiet. This obviously made it easier for Mr. Felser to identify the guilty parties. There were a few people who talked on occasion, including yours truly. The first time I got caught by Mr. Felser I picked up paper around the cafeteria along with a few other select individuals. The second time, I picked up paper and also scheduled a paddling for later that day. Mr. Felser knew me because I was in his industrial arts class. On that day, upon command (i.e., "Mr. Cipani, assume the position"), I got ready. Mr. Felser remarked, "Well Mr. Cipani, you are fortunate today, my wrist is a little weak." (thinking to myself: *well, please by all means hit me while you are weak. In fact, if you want to try to paddle me with just your pincer grasp around the paddle, I am all for innovation in discipline techniques Mr. Felser*) The blow came and it pushed me forward. Boy was I glad he was a little weak. I would have hated to catch him when he had his Wheaties for breakfast! No marks were left, but the hit was so hard that it jerked several tears from my eyes immediately upon contact. I went back to the next period. I was never called again for a violation of quiet time for the remainder of the year. Once was enough for me.

However, what was apparent to me at that time (and not having taken one psychology class) was that there was a small but distinct group of 7th and 8th grade boys who were called out constantly. I can remember the name of one of them, Mr. Leonard Tortelloni (not his real name). It seemed like it was every other day that Leonard was talking or doing something to gain the attention of Mr. Felser. One of his more devious ploys was to dump the contents of his tray, before it reached the disposal area (i.e., food and plates landed on the floor). What was also apparent to everyone was that Leonard did not try to violate the rule in a stealth fashion. He actually looked like he wanted to get caught. Was he not playing with a full deck?

Based on my personal experience, I wondered how he could handle such a paddling on a multiple time per week basis. Leonard had long hair and wore extremely tight pants, which was the style back then. I also knew that he and several of his fellow quiet time violators were quite popular with the girls. Do you see why Leonard and his band of brothers acted they way they did? They weighed physical pain versus later pleasure. I choose lack of pain and lack of pleasure. The "bad" boys saw this as a mark of honor, and they were lining up in droves for the paddling, and subsequently collecting phone numbers right after receiving their "punishment." I would also surmise that calling Mr. Tortelloni by name in front of the entire lunch shift was not a wise move either, on the part of Mr. Felser.

- Why was spanking not an effective punisher for Mr. Tortelloni?
- What could have been done to affect the behavior of Mr. Tortelloni?

While I had to experience the consequence only once to be a believer in quiet time, such a contingency only spurned Mr. Tortelloni to greater heights of mischief. Despite what you might have previously thought about paddling as being synonymous with punishment, in the case of Mr. Tortelloni and his friends, it was not. Of course, if an outcome-oriented definition is used, one would see that paddling Mr. Tortelloni is not punishment.

The outcome-oriented definition of punishment (Grusec & Walters, 1977) is the definition I will use for the remainder of the book. Punishment depends on the outcome of the contingency. If the procedural contingency produces a decrement in the behavior that is targeted, then punishment occurred. If does not, then punishment did not occur, irrespective of the noxious nature of the consequence.

Perhaps this example can make the distinction even clearer. If I asked you, "Is having a teacher hug a student a reinforcer or a punisher," many of you would emphatically state it is a reinforcer. Forgive me for putting words in your mouth, but your rationale for such an evaluation is most likely that hugs are an inherent sign of care and affection and therefore, should be considered a reinforcer. You probably can't see where getting a hug could be aversive, could you? But using the outcome-oriented definition, if a teacher hugs a child each time she says the correct answer to a problem and as a result the rate of correct answers decreases, we have punishment! I am sure you could now figure out some scenarios where hugging could result in the behavior it produces becoming less frequent. If you doubt this, start frequently hugging your teenager in front of his or her friends for some set of behaviors and watch those behaviors disappear from their repertoire! Now there is a discipline strategy I bet you never thought of before reading this book!

In the example offered in the introduction, what was the consequence for a child's aggressive behavior? If a child threw another child off the bike, he or she lost the opportunity to ride the bike for the remainder of the free play, as well as receiving a short time-out. Was the contingency (i.e., loss of bike time) a punisher? The answer, most definitely, is "Yes." Aggression was reduced when such a contingency was put in effect. Note that no physically painful event was needed to effect punishment of aggressive behavior in this case. It simply required the loss of the opportunity to ride the bike, contingent on aggression.

The outcome-oriented definition of punishment also leads to an important distinction. As a behavior analyst, I view punishment as something that occurs to a behavior. Contrast this with the common conception of punishment, i.e., you punish the person. This is a significant distinction. When I use punishment I desire to decrease a behavior by producing an effective behavioral contingency that alters that behavior. What is the objective when you punish a person? What behavior or behaviors do you intend to alter? Or is altering a behavior a concern at all? As a side note, the same mistake is often heard in reference to reinforcement (i.e., reinforce a person). If you hear someone claim they reinforce the child, tell them that people cannot get reinforced. How does one increase a person? Rather, a behavior is reinforced (i.e., strengthened in future probability). That should make you popular at your next social function!

Section II:
Exposing Myths About Punishment

Many attributions have been made over the years about punishment. Statements such as, "punishment does not work," or "punishment only serves to express anger on the part of the parent," have been cited frequently. These statements are taken as fact, without asking for substantiation of such claims.

For example, a speaker at a professional conference denounces the use of punishment as a tactic that does not work. Many people applaud, and cite the presentation as evidence that punishment does not work. This speaker's statement is taken as fact, not personal opinion. But where is the scientific evidence that demonstrates punishment procedures have been reliable failures in changing child behavior? On the contrary, many studies that I will present in this book provide evidence that punishment procedures are effective in changing a wide variety of behaviors. Many experts, however, have told us that it does not work. Who is one to believe?

Now suppose that same speaker said, "I have looked at your hand and it is blue!" You would not believe this statement because the evidence is staring you in the face. Your hand is not blue. In this situation you would weigh the evidence for and against the validity of the statement and conclude that it is not believable. Weighing the evidence, and the *credibility* of such evidence, is the key to detecting what is fact, from what is opinion.

I want to stress this point vociferously. Across all contentions made in defense of or in opposition to punishment, you should apply that "weighing the evidence" process. You should apply this level of scrutiny regardless of how many Ph.D.'s the speaker or author has behind his or her name. Parents and professionals need to discern which statements are based on research and which ones are based on either anecdotal tales, someone's perceptions about reality, or philosophical/moral positions. Evidence is evidence and opinion is opinion. Opinion does not equal scientific fact, regardless of the number of books someone has written. Too often, in the field of human behavior, opinion and perception have been disguised and paraded as fact.

In a book entitled, *Punishment and its Alternatives*, Drs. Johnny Matson and Thomas DiLorenzo reported that few well-controlled studies examining the effects and side effects of punishment have been conducted (Matson & DiLorenzo, 1984). This statement is just as true today as it was in 1984 (Lerman & Vorndan, 2002). Unfortunately, the prohibition against conducting basic animal research on punishment effects further impedes the acquisition of scientific data (Dinsmoor, 1998). Why is this lack of research examining punishment bad?

Lack of research leads to speculation. Speculation leads to the advent of myths and beliefs about behavioral effects of punishment. Over time, myths take on a level of believability as quasi-evidence. The erosion of factual evidence makes the myths appear to have a basis in fact. Such appears to be the case with many of the lay and professional writings on punishment and its effects.

There are several misconceptions that are frequently made about punishment and the use of it to produce child behavior change. Unfortunately, these commonly cited misconceptions have had a deleterious effect on the responsible use of punishment in situations where it may be warranted. Further it has had a stifling effect on applied research. For these reasons, such myths need to be exposed. The following five myths about punishment, I believe, have resulted in a misuse, lack of use and/or abuse of punishment:

- **Myth #1: Punishment Does Not Work**
- **Myth #2: Punishment Temporarily Suppresses Behavior (And Therefore Is Not Worth the Effort)**
- **Myth #3: Punishment Causes Problems for a Child's Emotional Development**
- **Myth #4: Punishment Is Not as Effective as Reinforcement**
- **Myth #5: Time-out Does Not Work**

Myth #1: Punishment Does Not Work

Why is this a Myth?

This statement is a myth for two basic reasons: (1) definition and (2) available scientific studies demonstrating effectiveness. First, by definition, outcome-oriented punishment always works, as was made evident in the previous section. Yet, how many times have you heard some parent, teacher or professional profess the following: "I have used time-out and it did not work. Time-out is a punishment technique. Therefore punishment does not always work. With some kids it might work. With others, it does not work."

I do not dispute that the use of time-out may not have been effective in the above situation(s). What is a technically correct conclusion is the following: Time-out did not function as a punisher, in this circumstance, for unknown reasons. Similarly, many people who have "grounded" their child may not have had success in changing their child's behavior. In these cases, grounding did not function as a punisher. As I would constantly tell my students, there are no inherent punishing events for everyone and every instance. In both these fictitious examples, one does not have outcome-oriented punishment. Rather, one has illustrated procedural punishment.

The second reason why this statement is a myth is that the applied clinical research data are overwhelming and compelling. There have been numerous research studies that have demonstrated that punishment can be effected by contingent applications of certain events and consequences. Further, such research is over a large range of behaviors with a wide diversity of children.

Claiming punishment does not work is akin to claiming airplanes cannot fly. Sure there are times when planes unfortunately crash. No one jumps up and says, "Hey those people who founded the principles of aerodynamics are wrong. See what happened to this plane." Anyone who claims that punishment does not work is either unaware of the numerous studies that have demonstrated the efficacy of punishment or chooses to ignore them. Showing anecdotal situations where a certain consequence (e.g., time-out) is ineffective, do not constitute "overwhelming" empirical evidence that a technique does not work. This is particularly true when the deployment of the technique is of an unknown entity. Perhaps it is the carpenter, not the tool, who is at fault!

How a plan is designed and implemented makes a big difference in its potential success. All carpenters are not equally competent. The following example illustrates why the specifics of a plan to change child behavior and a consistent follow-through are crucial in determining if some strategy will work.

It Will Never Work With These Kids!

In the early 1980s, I was involved as a behavioral consultant with a program for children with severe problem behaviors. These children were usually removed from the public school setting as a result of unmanageable behaviors. They were placed in a residential facility, where they lived and went to a school on the grounds of that facility (just for children with such problems). One of the teachers I had worked with mentioned a unique problem to me. She had a small class of young boys. She was concerned about the amount of food waste occurring during lunchtime. She said the children would often throw away more than half of their food. The teacher's perception was that the children were only eating the dessert and some portion of the other food. This occurred despite the fact the children were able to take as much or as little as they desired, in a cafeteria-style lunch. When I proposed that we design a behavior plan to address this problem, the teacher was skeptical. "It probably won't work for these kids. They are picky eaters by nature." But she agreed to give it a try.

We implemented a system to start measuring whether plate waste occurred for each student during the lunch period, so that consequences could be brought to bear (Lau & Cipani, 1984). Each child was to select a portion of vegetables and the main dish, at whatever amount he desired (as had been the case before). However, before he emptied the tray, the student was to show the teacher his plate. If it had food on it, the student did not earn points unless he went back and finished it. The points were to be traded in later for time on preferred activities. If the student had finished his food, then he earned three points for that effort.

Was the loss of not earning three points enough to change their wasteful eating habits, when other attempts had failed? Again remember, they only had to eat the amount, however small, of food they put on their plate. Waste was the issue. The use of such a consequence for food waste was implemented before and after a several week stretch where no consequences were deployed, to determine if consequences were effective. The results are depicted in the chart below for five male students. The percentage of food waste for the main dish is depicted as a function of the use of the consequence described above (see both columns marked Ind. Conseq.) versus the lack of such a consequence (column marked No Conseq.).

Student	Ind. Conseq.	No Conseq.	Ind. Conseq.
Jack	20	44	Not present
K. K.	0	20	0
K. M.	20	40	0
Vince	40	56	11
Wally	0	70	20

Look at Vince's data. He went from 56% of the lunches having food thrown away, to 11% (last column) when he would not earn points when he wasted food. Wally's data is equally impressive. When contingencies are in effect, his average rate of food waste is zero and 20% respectively. Look what happens when the only consequence was probably slight embarrassment (middle column). His food waste percentage goes to 70%. A similar finding for the effectiveness of consequences was obtained for the student's consumption of vegetables. Does somebody want to explain how this is an example of an ineffective procedure?

What is more impressive is to consider the context under which these results were obtained. Consider this anecdotal evidence. Several classes ate lunch during this time period. Only this teacher's class was using a consequence for wasting food. On my observations during the study, it was readily evident that students from other classes were wasting food, throwing large portions of their lunch in the trash bins. Don't we hear, on a regular basis, that children are influenced by their peers? Is it not an undisputed fact that children pick up bad behaviors from their peers?

For all of the talk about kids modeling each other's behavior, the results of this study may demonstrate the power of consequences over modeling effects. At the time of the study, it was not possible to set up a system for all children in the lunchroom at that time to not waste food. Nor did the other teachers appear to be interested in making food waste an issue. However, in spite of the fact that there was "negative" modeling of food waste, the students in this study wanted to earn points more than imitate their peers. Can consequences for behavior override negative peer influences? Examine this study and consider that possibility. Here is further food for thought. What are the implications for parents regarding their children's watching of violent TV or video programs and its supposed stimulus for aggression? Is it "automatic" that children will imitate what they see?

- What effect did the point contingency have on the food waste of the target students?
- Why were students not in this class unaffected by this point system?
- Do you think food waste is a problem at other schools?

Does Punishment Always Work?

Perhaps this seems like an indefensible statement if one conjures up a specific punishing event and attempts to explain how it would work all the time. I am not saying that spanking, or time-out, nor loss of special privileges, or other forms of consequences for child misbehavior always works. If we go back to the outcome-oriented definition of punishment that I am using, then by definition, punishment always works (to decrease a behavior). Certain applications of consequent strategies do not work under certain conditions. If one utilizes this definition of punishment, than certain applications may not work, hence punishment did not take place. Perhaps a hypothetical example can make this distinction more clear.

Let us say Betty decided to remove 10 cents (a fine) from her 14-year-old son's allowance for each chore he does not perform over the course of a week. She feels this will "punish him" for being lazy. (*Note to reader: remember the first tip is to understand that one punishes behavior, not people, in outcome-oriented punishment.*) His allowance is $8 for a week. His chores are raking the leaves in the front yard, emptying the house garbage cans in the dumpster twice a week, and cleaning his room on Friday. Her son rarely completes these chores. Betty pleads with him, threatens him, and then sends him to his room if she is really upset with him. When that does not work she proclaims that he takes after his father's side of the family, and his laziness is probably genetic! Hence, Betty has a strong desire to try something that will succeed in getting her son to complete his chores around the house.

For a 2-week period prior to the fining system for chores, Betty charted her son's completion of these chores. She told him, "Now I am going to be writing down whether or not you do your assigned chores or not. You better get on the stick." Her son was apparently unimpressed by having a permanent recording of his lack of performance posted on the wall. He continued in his old ways. He did not rake the leaves either week, he did not empty the garbage cans at all (four opportunities) and he did not clean his room. Again, this confirmed in Betty's mind that her son really is lazy. She remarked to herself, "What is it with 14-year-olds these days? They just don't care."

Following this 2-week recording period, Betty implemented the fining strategy for 3 consecutive weeks. Did this undo her son's genetic defect? The results were not impressive. His lack of attending to the chores resulted in fines for each chore, save one time when he took out the garbage in the first week. Betty concludes that her son does not respond to punishment. She remarks, "This proves that his father's genes are responsible for his laziness since he does not even care if he loses money. How can you be that lazy? Just like his father."

Obviously her strategy did not work, but is she wrong in concluding that punishment does not work for her son? The answer should be obvious. The correct conclusion from this hypothetical case is that removing 10 cents from her son for every uncompleted chore was a strategy that was an unfortunate failure. However, would the results have been the same thing if we "upped the ante" to maybe $1 for each uncompleted chore? What about loss of a dollar and loss of half an hour of TV time on the weekend for each uncompleted chore? Betty currently does not have an effective punisher in place for her son's chores, but the night is young! If she understands that punishment is defined in terms of its outcome, she might possibly refine the plan. She may increase the fine for chores or add other components to the plan to change her son's rate of completing chores.

So, by definition, outcome-oriented punishment always works. To determine whether punishment has occurred one looks after the fact. If the target child misbehavior was reduced as a result of the consequence, punishment occurred (up to that point). If the behavior did not become less probable, punishment did not occur.

What is the Utility of this Outcome-based Approach?

Obviously, we can all make better decisions about things after they have occurred. So, what good does this outcome-based approach have for real life? This is a good question and I have a good answer. My answer brings me back to my earlier university teaching days. The graduate students in my classes in the 1980s would often question an outcome-based definition as having any real life utility. When students would question the usefulness of such a definition, I would say, "If you see it this way, you will always hunt for a better mousetrap and not accept a defeatist attitude toward changing child behavior. To try something and conclude, "Well that did not work, I guess it is not meant to be," is all too common. However, if you understand that this specific application did not work, but altering the consequence in some fashion may produce results, you will persevere where others have already given up.

Let's take Betty's case again. If she concludes that punishment does not work, she stops the fine system. She then becomes even more depressed about her fate of having married someone who is passing on these bad genes. This is often accompanied by no intervention at all for some period of time, further perpetuating her feelings of helplessness. However, if she reasons that this one application did not work as intended, but knows that some other consequence may succeed, she proceeds to re-design her strategy for dealing with this behavior. She attempts to build a better mousetrap!

Betty might first try to increase the fine, as the current fining system only results in a loss of 40 cents a week if her son does absolutely nothing. Her son probably does not see such a consequence as a big deal, because he would still have $9.60 each week. That is too much profit for someone who does absolutely nothing. She also decides to focus just on room cleaning for now and become a little more exacting in the deadline for her son to clean his room. If his room is not clean by Thursday at 8:00 P.M., then he does not get to go out with his friends Friday afternoon after school, in addition to a heftier fine ($5 for an unclean room). Betty also spends time with him two Thursdays in a row teaching him what a clean room is. With these changes, Betty hits pay dirt. Her son cleans his room for the first 3 weeks of the program.

I would say that Betty has definitely made an impression on her "genetically defective" son. Armed with her understanding of how to use punishment and other procedures effectively, she can now tackle the other two chores in a similar fashion. Her son has demonstrated that he does take notice of a substantially larger fine, combined with possible loss of time with friends.

What Do You Call a Severe Consequence that Does Not Work as a Punisher?

An aversive situation for everyone involved! What is apparent is that outcome-oriented punishment does not exist. If a child is constantly subjected to time-out, in the range of 8-15 times per day, month after month, I would conjecture that no one is satisfied. It is certainly not in the child's best interests to be spending that much time away from pleasant activities. I am also certain that the parent is unhappy about having to engage in the time-out scenario that many times a day. If the number of time-outs is not reduced over time, as a result of a marked decrease in the child's target behavior, something is wrong in Cocoa Beach! Perhaps it is the random application of such a consequence for many behaviors. Therefore, an inevitable contingency does not exist. Or it could be that some of the other parameters of punishment are missing, such as the removal of a competing reinforcement contingency (see Section III for details). Lack of adherence to any of the basic principles delineated in Section III could be the culprit. But what we do know is that punishment is not operable, it is just an unpleasant situation for everyone.

Why is this Myth Perpetuated?

Two primary reasons: (1) poor applications of consequences that are incorrectly termed punishment, and (2) quasi-research. Let me start by explaining what I mean by poor applications of consequences. The use of positive reinforcement and punishment procedures to solve problems with children's behavior in schools and home settings began appearing in the professional literature in the 1960s. There were many studies demonstrating the utility of behavioral procedures to increase appropriate behavior and decrease disruptive behavior. The conduct of these studies was carefully controlled, in particular, the implementation of the treatment regimen. If the study was testing the efficacy of a point system on reducing tardiness in a class, then the contingent relationship between being tardy and losing points was assured. The implementation of the treatment regimen was strictly adhered to, often with extensive help from graduate and undergraduate "volunteers." One must realize that in the research literature, published studies were conducted with precision. The numerous validation studies that accumulated were demonstrations of model implementation. The treatment strategy was conducted like clockwork, and sloppiness was not an option.

But what would happen if the persons conducting these studies were sloppy in their implementation of the treatment procedures? What if instead of losing points every time a student was late, we had a smorgasbord of consequences that could be used? Sometimes five points would be deducted from the student's point total. Other times, if the teacher felt the student did not intend to be late, only 2 points would be deducted. Still, with other tardy instances, the teacher might feel compelled to give the student a lecture about the need to be punctual to class. If the student promises to "straighten up and fly right from here on in," the teacher lets the student off with a warning. Do you see where we are headed? Right to the child discipline strategies of many adults, who then claim that fining a child for misbehavior does not work! Again, they blame the tools. The tools, however, are fine in the right hands. It is the particular carpenter who is misusing the tools and needs further training on how to use these tools effectively. Below is an example of this smorgasbord approach to consequences.

Parent: Dr. Cipani. We have tried everything. Our daughter continues to throw tantrums when she does not get her way.

Therapist: I can see you are frustrated over this situation. Let me get an idea of some of the strategies you have tried. Give me some examples of your strategies in dealing with her tantrums.

Parent: We have used time-out, reasoning, prodding, warning, ignoring, pleading, and even spanking her. We have also sent her to counseling for a 7-month period, hoping that will help her. She does not realize that she cannot have everything she wants. (*Note to reader: Why would you think she continues in this manner. Might it be that tantrum behaviors eventually produce something from the parents? Hmm?*)

Therapist: Tell me more about time-out. Have you used it within the last two weeks?

Parent: Yes.

Therapist: What does she do when she has a tantrum?

Parent: She cries, whines, says hateful things and is generally "uncouth." If she wants a candy bar, and I don't give it to her, she will cry and say she does not love me, because I am mean.

Therapist: That does sound hurtful. Being a parent myself, hearing that has got to hurt to some extent. I know it must be hard to ignore that.

Parent: It sure does hurt. She knows that too. At some point in time she shows that she is sorry for what she said. When she does apologize for her remarks, which is quite often the case, I promise her candy later, for being sensitive.

Therapist: (*What did I just finish thinking? Throw a tantrum, say hurtful things, apologize and voila! Candy.*) That is interesting. (*I need to see whether she sticks to the time-out for each incident or applies it at whim.*) Let's slightly change direction for just a minute. How many times have you put her in time-out for the last two weeks?

Parent: I would say no more than five times. I try not to use it if I don't have to.

Therapist: (*That does not sound good.*) How many tantrums would you say she has had in the last 2 weeks?

Parent: Countless.

Therapist: Would you say more than 20?

Parent: Easily.

You can see that the efficacy of time-out in reducing this girl's tantrum behavior has not really been tested. Time-out occurs in only a small proportion of the tantrum incidents. What has been tested is a little bit of this and a little bit of that. Maybe Emeril can make Beef Stroganoff perfectly by trusting his judgment, but I would sure feel more comfortable when less trained cooks follow a recipe. It is important to realize that many judgments about punishment and reinforcement are from recipes of unknown entities, with people who have not had formal cooking lessons.

But there is a second factor that I believe maintains this myth about punishment. This second factor is what I call quasi-research. Much of quasi-research, which extols the horror of using punishment, comes from investigations that use parent interview as the primary or main source of the data collection. From this, conclusions about real life behavior are made. For example, one of the earliest research studies on children and parents was compiled in a book published in 1957 (Sears, Maccoby,

& Levin, 1957). The authors developed extensive interview procedures, asking mothers questions about their child and their parental methods of dealing with their child. Their study included hundreds of mothers being interviewed. This gives people the impression that their conclusions have to be right because so many subjects were part of the data collection effort. Their study attempted to find correlates between what the mothers reported they did with their children and the mothers' report about how their children behaved.

In one of their chapters on children's conscience, they conclude that higher levels of conscience in children are associated with love-oriented techniques (e.g., use of praise, reasoning, etc.). In contrast, lower levels of conscience development in children are associated with more materialistic parenting techniques. These techniques are the use of rewards, loss of privileges, and use of physical punishment. You can see where the dilemma is created. Many of the behavior analysis studies cited in this book reveal such parental contingencies work well in reducing target problem behaviors. The data cited in the behavior analysis studies resulted from an independent observer, who counted the frequency of the child's behavior. Hence, bias and perception were reduced to a minimum.

Which Studies Should Be Used to Judge the Efficacy of Punishment?

Unlike the parenting research by Sears and colleagues (Sears et al., 1957), the behavior analysis studies did not ask the parents how they thought the procedure might or did work, but rather they put it to the test. This is referred to as an experimental analysis of behavior. Of utmost importance, these studies allowed the researchers to make conclusions about what really works, instead of speculating about what works. For example, in our previously cited study (Lau & Cipani, 1984), the use of the fine system produced lower levels of food waste in students during lunchtime. In contrast, removing the punishment contingency resulted in food waste reaching heightened levels. We demonstrated a causal relationship between contingencies (or lack thereof) and the amount of child food waste.

According to the Sears interview data, we should not have achieved our successful results in reducing food waste! Use of a materialistic intervention, such as points backed up by tangible items, should not result in improvements in child behavior. According to Sears and colleagues, only love-oriented techniques are found to be correlated with better child behavior.

The conclusion you should draw— *not all research studies are created equal.* An experimental analysis allows researchers and readers of the research to conclude cause and effect. When you test the efficacy of a procedure against its absence and show that the level of misbehavior is a function of whether the procedure is in effect (or not), you have demonstrated causality. On the other hand, correlating how parents report they have raised their children with the child's level of behavior does not. Now you have a basis for believing one set of research findings over the other. The behavior analysis findings are more credible because of their analysis of cause and effect.

I have another problem with this type of correlation research. Asking people whether they think punishment worked or did not work for them when they were children is no way to build a base of knowledge. *A science of human behavior requires more than a Gallup Poll approach to posing questions about people's perceptions of effectiveness.* One does not determine the composition of the moon's atmosphere by sampling the public on their thoughts and perceptions about the moon.

Here is an illustration of the fallacy of correlation studies concluding causal relationships. Suppose a research study shows that children who eat peanut butter also have a greater tendency to wear fancier shoes. Common sense, would dictate that we not draw the inference that eating peanut butter causes children to dress better in terms of their shoe apparel, or vice versa. Showing that two things are associated does not mean they cause one another. No matter how tempting it is to invoke causality, you cannot! This is usually a principle taught in an introductory psychology class, but apparently forgotten by some of the people who pursue advanced degrees. Now that you have this distinction, in which body of research are you going to put more credence?

What Might Be an Alternative Explanation for the Sears et.al. Data?

Let's take for granted the accuracy of the self-report data, which I consider a huge leap in faith. Consider the following as a plausible conclusion. Children with high levels of conscience can evoke more pleasing behaviors in the adults who care for them. Concurrently, children who have high levels of misbehavior evoke lesser amounts of praise from adults. Does that not fit with what we observe in the world on a daily basis? If you had two teachers, one who frequently issued praise in her class and one who did not, what would you conclude? Is it possible that the rate of praise is a function of the students in the class? Do kids that follow instructions at a higher rate make it easier for teachers to provide them lots of praise? Is the opposite also true?

It is dangerous, in my opinion, to find an association between certain types of parental behavior and child behavior and assume that one causes the other. This is quasi-science; it looks like science, but it really has over stepped its limitations. This can be dangerous and lead to statements that can cause people to believe something that may be totally false.

Why is it Dangerous to Conclude Causality from Correlation Research?

In the 1950s and 1960s, mothers of children with autism were wrongly accused of creating their child's disorder by a psychoanalytic psychiatrist, Dr. Bruno Bettleheim (Bettleheim, 1967). He was quite well known, so his writings became widely disseminated on the topic. He noticed that the mothers of these children were cold and aloof to their child's behavior, unlike mothers of other children. He concluded that the mothers needed analytic therapy to help them overcome their personality defects, claiming they had a syndrome he called "refrigerator mothers." In his eyes, and the eyes of many that used his writings as gospel, these mothers caused their children to socially withdraw, not communicate and engage in stereotypic and ritualistic behavior. Bettleheim believed that if the mother would just be able to shed her refrigerator personality, the child would develop like other children, so he believed. Of course, the tragedy is that in addition to having a child with severe deficits, these mothers also were now made to believe and feel that they caused their child's disability. Shame, Shame!

We now know better. Having a child with autism creates an unusual circumstance, one in which attachment behaviors on the part of the mother are not reciprocated. Children with autism are withdrawn and often do not show the usual attachment and bonding type responses to their mothers. Dr. Bettleheim had the causal arrow going in the wrong direction. It wasn't the mothers who were causing the child's behavior. Rather, it was most probably the child's lack of affectionate behaviors that was a more plausible explanation of some mother's emotional distance to their child. By the way, many fathers have an even more difficult time with their autistic children, in my experience. I wonder why Dr. Bettleheim did not consider the possibility of freezer fathers?

What are Some Research Studies that have Experimentally Tested Punishment Procedures?

Making bus rides safe for everyone. What parent has not had difficulty with children during car trips? The noise level can sometimes be so elevated that car accidents become more likely. Now, consider that school bus drivers have usually a much larger number of children as they traverse the roads. A survey in Leon County, Florida, in the late 1970s revealed the seriousness of this problem (Greene, Bailey, & Barber, 1981). Twenty-five percent of the resignations of school bus drivers were reported to be a direct function of the bus driver's inability to manage or tolerate school bus disruptions. And you thought driving a school bus for a couple of hours is an easy job!

These researchers tested the efficacy of a unique punishing event (loss of music while riding the bus) on an extremely noisy afternoon bus route. The punisher, removal of music, occurred for frequent bursts of disruptive noise on the school bus. If the bus riders stayed below a certain number of incidents of disruptive noise on a given trip, they could have preferred music played the following afternoon while riding home on the bus. However, if they went above a designated target level of disruptive noise bursts, they lost the music on the following afternoon trip.

In order to accurately measure the decibel level of noise, an automated electronic system was used. The researchers instituted a sound recording device above the driver's head that could be adjusted so that when the noise in the bus reached a certain level, a light display, called Noise Gard, was activated. To insure that bus noises, such as rumblings and the drone of the engine did not set it off, a filter of 500Hz was set. A noise level at or below this would not register. The Noise Gard gave the riders feedback each time the noise level went above the designated target. Additionally, it kept track of each reading above the allowed decibel level as well as the length of time the noise level stayed above the criterion level. In this manner, each instance of heightened noise levels could be accurately determined right at the point of occurrence, by a machine.

The results demonstrated that a group of noisy bus riders could be taught to keep their noise down to a reasonable level. The removal of preferred music during the bus ride, as a consequence for noisy behavior, did the trick. (*Note to reader: This consequence, removal of music, is well within the realm of possibility for parents with noisy kids during short car trips.*)

Rule-following behavior in classrooms. Students who were referred to a special summer class by their teacher, principal, and school psychologist served as subjects for a study by Azrin and Powers (1975). These students demonstrated extreme disruptive behavior during the regular school year and grossly deficient academic skills. Could you imagine a class of students such as this? Take all the kids with severe problem behavior across an entire school district, and put them in one class. The teacher of this class should get combat pay and free mental health services!

How bad was the disruptive behavior in this special classroom? The rate of disruptions averaged 30 per child per day. Would informing these children of the rules do the trick? During the initial period of the study, the teacher repeated the rules for the class with each disruption. For example, if a child talked without being called upon, the teacher would remark, "Do not talk unless you are called upon." The teacher simply appealed to the child's sense of righteousness. Would that be enough to reduce disruptive behavior? Do pigs fly? Observing the class at that time revealed numerous instances of children walking and running about, talking, hitting other students and generally creating a lack-of-learning environment. Repeating the rules when students violated them was unfortunately, ineffective.

While it would be nice if the effective intervention for these children would be comprised of simply pointing out their misbehaviors, such was not the case. However, consequences often work where other strategies fail. How about if the student is required, during recess, to recite the rule and practice the correct classroom behaviors when she or he failed to follow the rules? Can anything help this teacher?

This consequence had a significant effect. The average level of disruptions per child was now about two. Dr. Azrin noted that the classroom now resembled an environment of learning. Children for the most part were considerate to each other, only left their seats with permission, and directed their attention to the learning activity. None of the children were shouting or walking about. When a child did leave his or her seat without permission it clearly appeared to be out of forgetfulness, rather than a deliberate violation of the rules, as it was in the past. Yes, Virginia. There is a Santa Claus for teachers. It goes by the name of "Effective Consequences."

Child behavior during shopping trips. A study, conducted by Dr. Rusty Clark, at the University of Kansas, had the following objective: to teach mothers how to manage the behavior of their children during shopping trips (Clark, Greene, MacRae, McNees, Davis, & Risley,1977). The mothers were taught a number of parenting behaviors in an advice package. They were taught to praise appropriate shopping behavior, keep the trips short in the beginning, and turn the shopping trip into a learning experience. The contingency aspect of this advice was a fine system, A.K.A., response cost. The children were each given a certain amount of money prior to the trip, listed on an index card (e.g., $1). The index card would have ten, $0.10 entries, thus equaling a dollar. The rules for the shopping trip were listed and reviewed each trip. For each violation, the mother merely stopped, pointed out the infraction, and deducted a dime from the stipend. Whatever money was left on the child's card could be spent on the next trip or saved. All parents participating in this study liked the advice package and found that it helped their children be more appropriate during trips. The results on disruptive behavior across all three families were as expected (i.e., marked improvements). How to use this advice package is detailed in my book (Cipani, 1999), *Helping Parents Help their Kids: A Clinical Guide for Six Child Problem Behaviors* .

Improving school attendance via fines. Response cost (A.K.A. fines) can also be used successfully in other areas where time-out is not feasible. How many schools have problems with student attendance? Is student attendance amenable to response cost consequences? A study addressed that question with a resounding, "Yes" (Alexander, Corbett, & Smigel, 1976). A residential facility served court ordered youth who engaged in repeated charges of truancy, assault larceny, unmanageable behavior, and probation violations. Seven of these students attended three local high schools. Baseline data revealed an attendance rate across all the classes in a 5-day period to be between 50-60% (a mean of 51%). Prior to the contingency, each student was given $1 for lunch, without any requirement on one's behavior. With the response cost contingency, the dollar for lunch was the fine for missing one or more class periods. A sack lunch would be provided to anyone who missed one class the previous day, instead of the dollar for lunch. You might say, "The day of the free cafeteria lunch is over!" With this change in policy, the average rate of attendance across all classes for the seven students rose to 80%. The average rate of daily class attendance rose even higher to 94% when any of the seven students who missed a class resulted in everyone missing a class, which is called a group contingency.

These researchers then tackled a second problem. They used a unique version of a response cost to curb coming back late from evening curfew in one of the female adolescent cottages. Prior to actual data collection, staff at the cottage reported curfew violations from the eight girls residing in this cottage to be a nightly occurrence. The designated contingency plan involved the following response cost. Coming home late resulted in a fine administered the following night in 15-minute increments. For example, if a girl came in 8 minutes late, she would have curfew moved up 15 minutes earlier the following night. If she came in 35 minutes late she would have a 45-minute earlier curfew time. The best results of this response cost procedure occurred with the following contingency. When everyone was responsible for coming home on time, lest *all* receive the appropriate amount of the fine, curfew violations reached zero minutes across all girls for almost half of the nights (7/15 evenings of perfect compliance with curfew). Who wants to stay out late now?

Can Parents Abuse Punishment?

Anyone who watches TV can see that abusive practices occur, and are often equated with punishment. But it is wrong to equate abusive practice with outcome-oriented punishment (O'Brien, 1989). One can use punishment and not be abusive. I feel that abusive practice is more often a function of an inept parental repertoire for changing the child's behavior. Nevertheless, in some other cases I think we are dealing with adults who loosely fit the criteria for adult and are clearly abusive for reasons other than not knowing any better.

In many of the circumstances in which I have been involved with through Child Protective Services (CPS), I have seen the following scenario. Typically the parent wants the child to do something. Because they are not able to get the child to comply with their request (as is the case many other times), they become extremely frustrated. They may try escalating the tone at which the child is told to do something, or get in the child's face, replete with facial grimaces and screaming. When that is to no avail, they hit. Unfortunately, hitting gets the kids attention this time, thus maintaining it as a more probable parental response for the next crisis situation. Subsequent to the spanking, the child moves and begins to comply. This is an unfortunate chain of events, because the physical response from the parent did produce movement on the part of the child, whereas other parental responses did not. However, the intensity of the hitting needed to get the child's attention increases over time, until it gets out of hand. Hence, this is not a path I recommend!

I believe that the parenting solution for child noncompliance is specific and consistent use of systematic consequences. What these parents need is a parental response that effects child movement much sooner, for both their sakes. Time-out, removal of points, guided positive practice, or loss of privileges (for a short period) can all be effective if the parent is taught how to act early in the compliance scenario. The majority of the parents I have dealt with through CPS did not intend to abuse their child. However, due to their inconsistent and inept use of any effective consequence, it was just a matter of time. It was a train wreck waiting to happen. The case below illustrates how things can get out of hand, but the key is the systematic use of a punishing consequence.

The Case of:

"I did not know what else to do—so I tied him to a chair!"

Take the case of Jerry and his mother. Jerry's mother had been referred to me as a result of severe problem behaviors in the home, leading to an unfortunate situation that caused CPS to be involved in this case. Jerry was not removed from his mother as a result of this incident, probably due to the lack of any sustainable injury. However, she was mandated to receive behavioral services and implement them with integrity.

Jerry was a 5-year-old boy with mild mental retardation. He also had extreme problem behaviors and high levels of activity. He was prescribed Ritalin and Clonidine for his hyperactivity. Some of the problems reported to my behavioral specialist assigned to this case during the initial assessment included frequent episodes of aggression to others, property destruction, abuse to self and noncompliance with parental requests. Additionally, he broke the leg of a neighborhood cat.

His mother reported that up to the incident when CPS became involved his behavior had become unmanageable. He would lose control daily, falling to the floor, kicking, screaming and hitting when either he was asked to do something or was told he could not have something he wanted. My behavioral specialist focused initially on compliance to parental commands. By reducing the level of noncompliance, often benefits to other problem behaviors accrue.

It was most probably a compliance situation on that fateful day. In our initial interview, it was apparent that Jerry's mother had minimal ability to effect compliance with any level of reliability. Observation of their interactions confirmed that suspicion. Here is a scenario that is representative of the events that transpired in Jerry's house (this verbal text is a facsimile for actual conversation).

Mom: Jerry, I want you to pick up your toys. (said in normal conversational tone)

Jerry: No, I don't want to do it.

Mom: Jerry, I really mean business. The behavioral specialist is here. This is what I need you to do. (In more forceful tone)

Jerry: No, I don't care about the behavioral specialist. (In much louder tone)

Mom: This is really upsetting me. You need to pick up your toys now or else. How would you like it if I take all your toys away (Now the voice volume is just below a scream)

Jerry: You can't do that! (Falls to the floor in anguish)

As you can see, each one challenges the other to exacerbate the intensity of the request or denial. It was rare that my behavioral specialist saw Jerry smile during the initial assessment phase. He always seemed angry. (*Note to reader: he probably figured he had to have his "game face" on all the time for whenever a request might be given.*) Well, one day, his mother said she just did not know how else to deal with him. He just became so unmanageable that she felt she had no other alternative but to tie him to a chair. Of course, this was observed by someone in the neighborhood and reported. Hence, her current situation.

Our approach was to understand that Jerry's mother needed to learn how to consistently implement a strategy. She probably did not intend to go to the lengths she went to that day. However, she just did not know what else to do. The plan designed was the following:

1. Present a command to Jerry, simple and straightforward, in normal conversational tone.
2. Do not scream with him during his tantrums.
3. Each time he complies he gets a check.
4. When he has earned three checks, he gets a preferred activity or item for a period of time.
5. Failure to comply results in a "sit and decide" period (i.e., Jerry would have to sit until he decided to comply with the task).

After my behavioral specialist demonstrated this three-check system and the sit and decide procedure with Jerry, his mother followed through with the plan. The results were increased compliance from Jerry, with a minimal need for his mother to have to use sit and decide. Jerry probably figured out that it was to his advantage to comply early, where he could get a check–waiting just meant he would have to comply any way without getting credit. My behavioral specialist's observations revealed that the whole situation had improved dramatically. He also noted that Jerry started laughing, and seemed to be at ease in his new environment. We believe both Jerry and his mother are happier now and better off. Punishing Jerry's noncompliance was essential to this mother-son relationship. Further, developing this repertoire in Jerry's mother reduced the possibility that she would resort to abusive behavior in the future.

- Why do you think Jerry's mother escalated her request when he initially failed to comply with her instruction?
- How important was it to increase Jerry's compliance to his mother's instructions?
- Do you know families where the children's behavior affects their relationship with their mothers and/or fathers?

In California, a state statute prohibiting the use of aversive techniques in schools was passed into law in 1993 (California Education Code of Regulations, 1993). This legislation was the outgrowth of abusive uses of "punishment" by some teachers in special education. An example of the "punishments" administered was a teacher who pinched the misbehaving student, by grabbing the student's skin and twisting it. I know of no research study that has investigated such a procedure. When people start improvising their use of consequences beyond common reason, we have trouble! It is for this reason that I advocate that certain consequences that have been verified as effective should not be used without due consideration, and even then only with expert consultation.

Additionally, the use of reinforcement for some appropriate behavior is imperative, as well as is the removal of specific reinforcement for target behavior. Techniques that produce their effect by removing reinforcement when the target behavior occurs have been demonstrated to be quite effective and are the preferred consequences from my perspective. While time-out is probably the most popular of these techniques, there are other consequences that capitalize on reinforcement and punishment working hand in hand.

Are There Risks if Parents Do Not Use Punishment?

What would you guess would be the state of affairs for Jerry in elementary school if his behavior had not changed? I have seen too many kids not succeed in school. It is my judgment that many of these kids are intellectually capable. Rather, their misbehavior occurs because they were never taught how to follow instructions of adults with any reliability. Dr. Daniel Goleman's 1995 book, *Emotional Intelligence*, deals with just this topic. Ask any teacher what the prognosis for educational success would be for a child who refuses to do his assigned work on a daily basis.

The greatest "life risk" these children face is that their misbehaviors are not dealt with effectively. They are at risk for not succeeding later in life when adults fail to change critical child problem behaviors at an early stage of their genesis. A child's noncompliance to parents at age 3 and 4 can lead to more severe forms of oppositional behavior, such as anger rages, at age 6, 7, 12 and so forth. While some parents may not see any problem with their child throwing fits of rage, other people will (e.g., teachers, neighbors, and other adults who come in contact with the child). To not intervene in an effective manner does not sound like a good plan to facilitate a child's development into a responsible adult.

One of the thoughts behind inaction on the part of the parents is the idea that their son/daughter is just going through a phase. "Oh, he's just going through the "terrible two's." I have had kids with severe behavior problems, who apparently went through the terrible 2's, 3's, 4's and they are getting ready for the terrible 15's. To believe that a child will just grow out of these problem behaviors just isn't the case with many kids. It may happen every once in awhile (*most probably due to the efforts of some teachers who take on this role of teaching appropriate behavior and consequating inappropriate behaviors when the child enters school*). But it is not something to bank your child's future on. Let's wait and see what happens next year, when he gets older, does not constitute adequate professional advice.

The Case of: "If I could turn back the hands of time."

Sometimes it is wise to listen and learn from people who have been through child rearing and have learned what not to do from experience. I wish I had a quarter for every time I heard something along the lines of the following, "Boy do I wish I could turn back the hands of time." Here is an example of one mother I was working with, who had two children who were far apart in years. Her oldest child was either a junior or senior in high school, while her younger child was in early elementary school. I was called in to teach her how to manage her younger child who had high rates of noncompliance to her instructions, who would tantrum when he did not get what he wanted (and so forth). She was doing quite well with the recommended behavioral plan, teaching her child the consequences of complying with her requests (and of course what happens when you do not comply). She could see that this strategy was working and she put her heart and soul into this plan.

Having seen how her older son behaved around the house, I hypothesized why she was so vigorous in her use of the compliance training procedure. My intuition was pretty much on the money when she and I had a conversation one day. She made a remark to me of the following nature: "If only you were around when my older son was growing up. What I did not know could fill a book. I made so many mistakes and I wish I could take them back." Her older son was having extreme difficulty in high school and was belligerent at home. Yes, it is too bad that we can't turn back the hands of time. Maybe things would be different from the way they have turned out. Unfortunately, in life some mistakes cannot be undone. But let's not try to rely on a plan that repeats them over and over again.

- Why would some parents have difficulty providing specific behavior guidelines and consequences for their child?
- Is it too late for this parent to change her older son's behavior?

How many of you would volunteer for surgery tomorrow just to see if everything that should be there is there? If you are in good health I assume your answer might be along the following lines: "Heck, no. Use some other technique to verify the status of my organs." Of course the intrusiveness of the surgery is far too great to be considered for a simple check up. However, let's change the situation. Suppose you get shot with a bullet in the chest. Are you now willing to have the emergency staff open you up to save your life? You see, one must consider the risks at the particular time when evaluating what is in the best interest of the person.

Using certain punishing aversive consequences is not something that should be lightly considered, particularly if one is only concerned about a minor problem. However, if I ever get shot, I would certainly waive my right to be free from intrusive surgery if it meant living. In the example below, someone did not take into account the dangerousness of the situation facing the individual.

Doing Nothing is a Risky Venture?

One of the greatest miscarriages of doing nothing was a case of an adolescent male in a state hospital for the developmentally disabled. I was called in to consult with the staff at the hospital for a serious behavioral problem. If you are squeamish, I apologize for the following description of his life-threatening problem. On two prior occasions and more recent to my consultation, this individual took a staple and scratched the underside of his penis, the length of the shaft. Blood was everywhere, and he was rushed to emergency at the hospital and fortunately survived this incident.

I attempted to make sense of his behavior. What purpose or function might such a behavior serve? I drew up a number of treatment procedures, based on several hypotheses about the possible function of the behavior. Does he do this to get attention? Maybe he does this to protest something that happened to him. One of my theories was that this incident was a mishap of a behavior that was probably occurring more frequently. He had scaly skin, on his leg, which was probably itchy. My hypothesis was that he would use some instrument, or whatever he could get his hands on, to scratch the dead skin off. One thing to keep in mind, he is not terribly communicative due to his developmental disability, thus hampering his ability to tell staff what the problem is (e.g., "Hey I have itchy skin here. Can I have something to scratch/relieve the itch?").

To address this hypothesis, I designed a plan that would teach him to use a shower brush for scratching the leg. In this manner, if his skin needed scratching, this would do the trick. Further, the disastrous result that occurred with the staple, even with a slip of the shower brush would be improbable. However, you must realize I was shooting in the dark, so to speak. The evidence pointing to any of the hypotheses was weak. This one made the most sense to me, upon examining all the evidence. But what if I missed the boat? What if I was wrong about this behavior's function? Then giving him a shower brush would obviously not take care of the problem. We would still have him scratching himself with the staple, with potential disastrous consequences.

I wanted to cover all possibilities, in light of the seriousness of the situation. I remember telling the hospital psychologist that my plan also called for a punisher if he was even caught with a single staple, since we most certainly knew he did not intend to staple papers together. My statement at that time was, "If my hypothesis about this behavior is wrong, I will at least feel that the use of a punisher will make the behavior less likely. In other words I did not want to put all my eggs in one basket, this person's life may have depended on my being correct.

The plan for the use of punishment was the following: If he was caught before the act or during the act, I wanted him to receive a consequence involving some extremely aversive smell, taste or sensation. While I know some of you may be inquiring, "why do that," there is research data to support the use of contingent aversive tastes/smells to decrease target behavior, particularly with individuals in institutional settings. Again, my approach was to cover all bases, including the reinforcement of appropriate behavior and the teaching of new adaptive behaviors.

I submitted the lengthy written plan, which called for the enactment of all parts. I left the consultation and the hospital administrator thanked me for my input. That was the end of my involvement. I called up the psychologist several weeks later, not being on the consultation anymore but obviously concerned about the case, and inquired about the client's progress. To my dismay and horror, nothing had changed. Someone on the human rights committee was concerned about the individual's right to be free from aversive tastes or smells as part of the punishment plan. What about his right to not have to be checked into an emergency room in a life-threatening situation.

What was missing here is perspective. Taking risks is relative. When you are pretty comfortable, you need not take risks. But if your situation changes drastically, risks of treatment have to be weighed against the ramifications of the continued maintenance of the problem. I would venture to say that most people would not like to have to receive injections on a daily basis. But people with diabetes subject themselves to this intrusion every day. Risk is relative.

- Why would the plan (i.e., to give him a brush for his scaly skin) not work if my hypothesis (regarding the behavior's function) was inaccurate?
- What are other circumstances in everyday life where risk is relative to benefit?

The risk of not intervening effectively with child problem behaviors is far greater than some of the purported risks of using punishment. The next time someone says to you, "Aren't you worried that using time-out will pose problems," you should make the following reply. "Not as worried as having my 7-year-old son fail to learn how to behave in a nonaggressive manner on the playground." That risk is too great, and using time-out will be far outweighed by the benefits of having him learn to play appropriately with other kids on the playground.

Myth #2: Punishment Temporarily Suppresses Behavior
(And Therefore Is Not Worth the Effort)

Isn't It Common Knowledge that Punishment Only Works Temporarily?

An often-stated characteristic of punishment is that the effect on the behavior being punished is only temporary (i.e., punishment merely suppresses behavior). Therefore, punishment is not worthy of consideration as a strategy, since it does not work in the long run.

This misconception is exemplified in the following hypothetical illustration involving a daughter's frequent disrespectful comments toward her mother. Let's say Mrs. Rodriguez decides to take action in the following manner. She will fine her 11-year-old daughter, Holly, a quarter each time she is disrespectful to her. On Sunday night, Mrs. Rodriguez tells Holly that any disrespectful comments made to her will cost Holly a quarter from her $5 weekly allowance, beginning tomorrow. Mrs. Rodriguez begins the behavioral plan on Monday. After breakfast, Mrs. Rodriguez asks Holly to get her backpack ready for school. Holly says, "stop bossing me around, I am old enough to know when I should get ready!" Mrs. Rodriguez calmly informs Holly that her disrespectful comment cost her one-quarter and she goes to the chart to cross out one quarter from her allowance chart. This generates a caustic outburst from Holly, "You rotten ****, you can't treat me like that!" Instead of getting flustered like she had in the past, Mrs. Rodriguez simply goes to the chart and crosses out another quarter. This pattern of disrespectful comments by Holly, with subsequent fines of one quarter for each incident, persists another three times. Holly apologizes before getting on the bus for school, but the fines *stick*.

After 2 weeks, Holly's disrespectful comments have decreased from about 3-5 per day before the plan was in effect, to less than one every two days. With this improvement, Mrs. Rodriguez feels Holly has learned her lesson. She has become a more feeling, caring daughter and has seen the error in her ways. (*Note to reader: if I had a dollar for every time I have heard this!*) She informs Holly that starting next week the fine program will be discontinued. It is up to Holly to "think before she opens her mouth." Do you believe that Holly has become a new person? Will Holly accept her responsibility to treat her mother with the same respect she wishes to receive?

If this were a movie, the answer might be "yes." As you might guess, too often the scenario is more like the following. Holly's use of disrespectful comments starts to increase until she is once again an impudent child, according to her mother. Her mother and her friends surmise that this behavioral plan did not work, since Holly is still being disrespectful. But was it a failure? I think not. The failure was in not keeping a good thing going!

Note that when the parent implements the punishing consequence each time the behavior occurs, the behavior becomes less frequent. In some cases in my experience, it disappears for long periods of time. When Holly was fined each and every time she made a disrespectful comment to her mother, the occurrence of such comments went down dramatically. However, once the possibility of a fine was removed, disrespectful comments began to reoccur, eventually wiping out the progress made previously. Thus, many people point out that the short-term effect of the punishing consequence (i.e., the fine) is negated once the adult halts its use. Therefore, the implication is that parents should find something else that produces a long-term effect. My retort is, "And what would that be?"

Is this a Valid Criticism of Punishment?

No, absolutely not! As the previous scenario shows, effective consequences do decrease a child's behavior. Whether it produces long lasting change is debatable at this point of the research.

However, for argument sake, let me consider the premise that punishment is only able to reduce or eliminate a behavior while it is in effect. Is this a sufficient reason to not consider its use in child behavior management? Perhaps an answer to this criticism of punishment can best be addressed by the following illustration. Suppose the state government decides to remove the monetary fine from traffic tickets. Since punishment purportedly only suppresses behavior, we should remove fines for traffic violations and come up with something better. As some self-proclaimed experts would have you believe, perhaps having the police officer catch the rule violator and appeal to his/her sense of duty or logic and give the explanation of the possible consequences of reckless driving. This would be would be just as effective, right? Not! As you can imagine, the number of infractions would increase dramatically! Neither you nor I would feel safe on the roads anymore. Anyone who has lived on this planet as an adult would not seriously entertain removing monetary fines as a consequence of breaking the traffic laws in favor of having police discuss the potential for endangering lives due to traffic violation behavior.

Would we then conclude that fining people for traffic violations is ineffective, because once you remove the law allowing for police to issue a fine, people start violating traffic laws! I think most people would conclude the opposite: The fine system does work, and it needs to be in place to control the rate of traffic violations. Without it we would have mayhem on the streets. One would not object to the use of the traffic fine as a consequence, on the grounds that it merely *suppresses* drivers' unlawful road behavior. If fines keep people in line while they are in effect, they are necessary in the effort to get people to drive according to the law and to save lives.

When you cut in line at a theme park, and get caught, you can be ejected from the park. It is this consequence, and the threat of its use, that most probably keeps such behavior down to a minimum. Would you want to go to a park that would just inform those transgressors that they have probably hurt the other people's feelings? Not unless you enjoy verbal and physical altercations with your fellow human beings, in which case some reality TV show is looking for you. Again, one would not see the use of ejecting people from the park, who are caught cutting in line, as a punishing consequence that only is effective for the short-term. Its continued use would be mandated by park officials and the overwhelming majority of the paying public alike.

Are we expecting too much from any intervention, when we desire that intervention to "cure" the child from engaging in the prohibited behavior after deploying such procedures only 3 times, 10 times, or for 2 weeks? What is the logic in thinking that a misbehavior the child has engaged in for 6 months will go away for good, in just 1 week, when parents use a persistent discipline strategy, no matter what that strategy is? Have we cured depression with a 1-week program?

I often tell parents there are usually no miracles in getting children to change long-standing misbehaviors that put them in conflict with their environment. I proceed by first figuring out what will reduce such behavior in the next week, see if it works, and continue it if it does. Once the parents and I have solved the short-term problem (i.e., getting an immediate change in problem behavior), then we move to solving it in the longer term. Let us not put the cart before the horse, so to speak. Our first job is to get a change in the behavior as soon as possible. Let's worry about what we are going to do 3 months from now when we cross that bridge.

What is the Scientific Basis for the Argument that Punishment Produces Only Temporary Results?

In 1944, Estes published a study that used rats (the animal) to determine the effects of a punishing event, such as electric shock, on bar pressing behavior. He first trained rats to press a bar, and reinforced this behavior with food pellets. Once the bar press response was developed, Estes then proceeded to continue putting the rats in the cage, except that two events were altered. First, a bar press no longer resulted in a food pellet (called extinction or removal of reinforcement). Additionally, an electric shock was delivered each time the rat pressed the bar. Therefore, when the rat pressed the bar, no food was delivered and a shock was presented instead.

These two conditions were in effect for the first 10 minutes of each training session. Of course, during these 10-minute periods, rats desisted from pressing the bar. Subsequent to this 10-minute session, the rat was removed from the cage for a short period of time. The rat was then placed back into the cage. During this second training period, only the lack of food delivery for bar press occurred (called the post test session). The question becomes the following: Will the rat press the bar during this non shock period, since s/he had received contingent shock just a few minutes ago? In other words, will the effect of the shock extend to a period where no shock is used? Rats in this posttest session behaved just like rats that had not been exposed to shock and began pressing the bar, with the result being only the lack of food delivery.

As a result of this experiment and ones similar to this, behavioral researchers at the time concluded that punishment is ineffective in modifying a behavior that was previously reinforced. They reported that punishment only suppresses behavior and that removal of the punishment consequence results in the behavior reappearing. As a side comment, it is important to note that in these experiments, bar pressing was the only behavior taught to the rats that produced food. Suppose the animal was taught that another behavior produced food (e.g., calling Pizza Palace), while bar pressing still resulted in shock and no food delivery. What might the results have been then?

Doesn't the Estes Study Prove that a Temporary Effect of Punishment is the Norm?

First, one should not make conclusions beyond what a study allows for. What did the above study (and similar laboratory studies at the time) actually show? The Estes (1944) study demonstrated that the punishing effects of shock, contingent upon the rat's bar press response, did not extend to a period shortly after each 10-minute training session. Can we then jump to conclude that the same short-term effect would have occurred if the rats had received punishment for bar pressing for a 3-month continuous period? Does a study that utilizes short periods of pairings of the punisher with the response allow one to generalize the findings to everyday life and conditions? Suppose a consequence is consistently applied for a proscribed child behavior for weeks or even months. Will it return once the consequence is terminated? In some cases, probably so. In other cases, I think not!

The existing data from these laboratory research studies do not provide a clear answer to this question, because they were so limited in scope. What conclusion I would find credible regarding the rat studies cited above is that if you punish a behavior for ten minutes, it may not generalize to a period after that where punishment is made unavailable. So if you want to cure your child of lying in the next ten minutes for the rest of his life, you are probably going to be disappointed with the result. However, I do feel that there is considerable clinical evidence that long-term effects can occur with an established contingency.

The Case of: "Stealing is in His Blood!"

In some cases, a behavioral pattern of long-standing nature can be addressed via a plan that incorporates punishment of the proscribed target problem behavior and reinforcement of its absence. A foster family I was involved with had several children, all of them coming from the same mother. One of the boys (Roberto, who was 9 years old at the time) had multiple problems. Further, he had not shown any progress in developing a "conscience" in the year he had resided in his new home. One of the most serious problems was stealing money and various things from family members as well as from classmates at school. This was apparently a behavioral pattern he picked up early in life. His biological mother felt her children should fend for themselves, hence his early exposure to shoplifting. I would imagine you could guess why he and his siblings were removed from their mother.

This behavioral pattern obviously distressed and annoyed the new foster parents. His foster father in particular was adamant about teaching him that this was wrong. Due to his early exposure to stealing food in order to eat, he had developed into quite and adept (and frequent) usurper of other people's possessions.

Prior to my involvement, the foster father had tried many strategies to rid Roberto of his stealing behavior. He tried pleading with him, discussing society's prohibition against stealing, appealing to his better judgment, trying to induce guilt and shame over stealing others possessions, grounding him, and other strategies. Unfortunately, none of these worked to eliminate this behavior. The father was in angst over each new episode of Roberto taking something from either a family member or getting a call from school regarding theft. It was essential that I design a plan to accomplish a short-term dramatic reduction of stealing. His current placement was in jeopardy, as both his foster father and his wife had doubts about their keeping Roberto. Further, I could not imagine that any other family would love to have a child that transfers possession of property from somebody else to himself. The only place I know that accepts these types of children is- you guessed it.

The plan I came up with was borrowed from several researchers at Florida State University (Switzer, Deal, & Bailey, 1977). It involved planting items around the house in conspicuous spots to monitor stealing (I called this the planted item technique). Each day the father would place several items, including money, in designated places (unannounced to Roberto). This allowed his father to systematically track stealing by checking each place where something was left, in addition to the usual check procedures.

Roberto was informed of the plan the night before it was to go into effect. If all the items remained in their place at the end of the day and there were no other reports of stealing, Roberto received $.50 for the day. However, if something was missing, the punishing consequences involved the following: (1) return item(s) stolen, (2) lose the stipend amount for that day, and (3) pay a penalty equal to double the value of the item(s) taken. Note that this plan had consequences for stealing as well as for not stealing. I believe the father also threw in early bedtime as well.

As you can imagine, his rate of stealing went down. In a several week period, he was no longer stealing, and this was also confirmed at school. Stopping this behavior had a profound impact on Roberto's position with his foster parents. Probably one of the nicest outcomes of changing Roberto's behavior happened on one of my visits to the home. His foster mother was so proud of him. In the earlier part of the week, Roberto had returned some planted money to her, saying he found it (planted item) and that she must have lost it. She thought he had finally turned the corner on his past! He had become someone who had a conscience.

Roberto also improved in other areas. His foster parents had misgivings about his placement early on as a result of his mischief when they had to hire a baby-sitter to go out together. He had several people quit, and these were people in their 20's. The mother's note to me on one instance early in the behavioral program illustrated this problem. "My husband and I went to a class at the junior college. The baby-sitter became so frazzled that she had to call my parents (who live nearby) to come over and calm him down. He was yelling at her, saying he did not have to listen to her." The last sentence of this note said, "Please help us with this boy."

To handle the baby-sitting crisis, we instituted a plan that was similar to one designed for him at school. This one was called the baby-sitter report card. Verbal refusal, aggressive attempts or postures, and leaving the house were three behaviors that we held Roberto accountable for while his parents were out of the house. The baby-sitter merely had to mark if either of these occurred. When his parents came home, if the baby-sitter reported on the card that one or more incidents of the above three behaviors occurred, he went to bed early that day and the next. With this plan, these behaviors rapidly disappeared. The real test of its efficacy can perhaps be seen in the increased number of new baby-sitters the parents could now deploy. Whoever has the report card has Roberto's attention. The baby-sitters hailed, "The day of fearing Roberto is over!"

About a year and a half later, I became involved with this family for another child in their care. They reported to me that Roberto had not had a problem with stealing since the last time I saw him and the program had been discontinued some time ago. It is important to remember that although he now demonstrates responsibility, the change in behavior was initially the result of a behavioral plan that rewarded him for not stealing, along with a severe penalty for stealing. He also had continued improvements in those other areas.

- What are the similarities between the designated plan for stealing and the behavioral plan developed to deal with the baby-sitter scenario?
- Do you believe that some children learn to steal at an early age? How so?

Is there Any Research Evidence that Punishing Effects Are Not Always Temporary?

As I indicated previously, there is unfortunately an insufficient research base to allow a scientific response to this question. If punishment effects can extend beyond their use, we currently do not know the factors involved that make long-term effects more likely. It is apparent that some children need their parents to follow through with the plan for months before even considering partially removing it. However, in many such cases, the punishing consequence is only rarely needed, since the rate of problem behavior is low or non-existent. A research study that targeted dangerous infant behaviors is a good illustration of the effectiveness of a punishment consequence in reducing the rate of behavior to low levels (Matthews, Friman, Barunc, Ross, & Christophersen, 1987).

Researchers at University of Kansas, under the direction of Dr. Mark Matthews, worked with parents whose infant children, at or under 1 year of age, displayed potentially dangerous behaviors. Such behaviors included playing around the wall socket, being in an area where the child could fall, or other similar hazardous conditions for the infants. Any parent can relate to this serious problem area. All four parents had tried to simply remove their child from the danger area (often called re-direction).

As many parents will tell you, simply moving the infant in another direction does not work. Many infants will continue to go back after being re-directed, thus necessitating continued vigilance on the part of the parent. It is unfortunate, but true, that many infants do not learn to avoid the hazard or danger, with this commonly accepted practice. While the technique is certainly something that no one would find objectionable, it also is ineffective. Hence, a technique that develops the infant's active avoidance of the danger condition, because of an effective punishing consequence, is required.

All four parents were taught to use time-out for their infant child. Immediately upon the child entering the danger condition, the parent was taught to say "no," place the infant in the playpen, and wait until she or he was quiet for 5-10 seconds. In addition these parents were also given specific suggestions by the trainers on child proofing those hazards in their home that represented potential danger.

During the baseline, the parents were instructed to intervene (i.e., re-direct the child) when they thought it was needed. This strategy could then be compared with the time-out procedure in its effectiveness. The table below provides the dramatic contrast between baseline and the use of time-out on each infant's percentage of time in hazard conditions.

Infant	Baseline	Time-out	%Change
1	55%	6%	49%
2	32%	3%	29%
3	35%	10%	25%
4	37%	4%	33%

The percentage of intervals the infant spent in potentially hazardous situations is significant before treatment. For example, infant 1 spent 55% of the time observed in hazardous situations. Note the low rate of all the infants being in a potentially dangerous situation when time-out was in effect. Infant 1 went from 55% before training to 6% after his parent started using time-out.

As I indicated previously, the mark of an effective consequence is that it reduces the rate of the target behavior to such a low level that the consequence rarely has to be deployed (Perone, 2003). Such was the case in this research study. Both infants 2 and 4 had 5 consecutive days during which the mother did not have to use time-out even once, since the infant never approached the hazard area! We would all agree that getting a child to learn to avoid the situation, with the advent of time-out available, is much more effective than constantly re-directing the infant.

These researchers revisited these 4 families 7 months after the termination of parent training (called a follow-up assessment). They observed the infants to see if they had continued to avoid the identified hazard conditions. Three of the four children (now between 17 and 19 months of age) did not receive one time-out during the observation period. One child did receive one time-out. All the mothers reported that they eventually liked the time-out and used it. This anecdotal finding was important information since some of the mothers reported they were distressed at their child's initial crying during the first few time-outs. When a punisher works, it often is the case that the child does not engage in the behavior that produces it: a pleasing state of affairs for everyone!

Another possibility in attempting to produce long-term results is to gradually remove the punishment contingencies by fading the daily use of such. How this fading procedure can be accomplished was the target of a research study conducted at a facility called Achievement Place (Bailey, Wolf & Phillips, 1970). This facility housed children who were delinquent and court adjudicated. One of the techniques developed in this research program was called the Daily Report Card (for detailed presentation, see Cipani, 1999). Each student was monitored as to his study behavior at school and rule violations. The teacher filled out the card for two questions: (1) did the child obey the classroom rules (Yes or No) and (2) did the child study the whole period (Yes or No). If the child had both questions marked with a Yes, he got special privileges at home that evening. If he had even one No, then he lost all privileges that evening and had to do extra chores to earn them back.

As you might imagine, with the possibility of losing privileges, the boys managed to increase their attention to their schoolwork during the two math periods the program was in effect. Further, the rate of rule violations become non-existent on most days and minimal on others.

In a last experiment in a series of experiments, the researchers tested the efficacy of a fading program. The report card would go home only on Tuesdays and Fridays of each week. The teacher could mark the card for incidents that occurred in between. For example, if the child had a rule violation on Monday, the Tuesday report card reflected that fact. The results indicated that for both rule violations and study behavior the impressive gains made for the daily reporting system were maintained with this faded system of twice per week over a 22-day period.

How Long Does a Parent Need to Use a Punisher Before Its Effects Become Enduring?

I unfortunately do not have a magical number because each child and family are unique. Parents must realize that the deployment of any behavioral plan probably needs to be maintained for longer than 2-3 weeks. The child's problem behavior may have a several month to several year history of development. Therefore the effort to change it has to be of some reasonable time period. I often give parents this piece of advice: "This behavior did not get here yesterday and it probably won't disappear from sight tomorrow."

Let's take the hypothetical case of Jack. Jack would make mean comments and remarks toward his sister, e.g., "You are stupid." His parents decided to use early bedtime as a consequence for mean remarks to his sister. Each time Jack told his younger sister that she was dumb or stupid, or when he called her ugly, he received a negative check mark on the calendar. If Jack had two check marks on a given day, he went to bed a half hour early. Of course his sister gets to stay up until regular bedtime, if she did not retaliate. If he had 3 checks he went to bed 1 hour early. More than 3 checks in a day, he went to bed right after supper. As you might imagine, the number of days he went to bed early, in the first 3 weeks of the plan, were few and far between. This represented a dramatic improvement in his mean remarks to his sister. His parents continued the program for the next 5 weeks. On the 12th week, Jack's parents made the following changes: one comment results in one hour early bedtime, two or more comments result in going to bed after supper. Again, Jack learned to control his "mean-spirited" behavior as a result of these consequences.

How long should Jack's parents carry out this plan? If Jack's behavior has occurred for about a year, his parents might consider keeping the initial plan intact for an additional several month period. If Jack's progress on this behavior is maintained across that time period, the parents might then consider altering parts of the plan. Changing child behavior is a race for distance runners, not sprinters!

The Power of Parental Consequences-
the Case of Getting Dressed

In some cases, a consequence is so powerful that its use becomes so infrequent, because the target behavior stops occurring. One of my behavioral specialists was working with a family of a girl who hated to get dressed in the morning. Every morning she would complain that she did not like the clothes set out for her. Her mother would give her another choice, however, the *battle royale* would often not stop there. She found the new version equally distasteful and the argument over what to wear to school would resume. The mom reported that this back and forth arguing, yelling, and tantrumming about getting dressed occurred every morning.

Observation by the behavioral specialist revealed that such an interaction was a morning ritual between mom and daughter.

Fortunately for us, this girl was addicted to TV, which apparently was considered a constitutional right in this home (at least this was the belief of the girl). The behavioral plan was simple: require her to change her clothes five times a day. Each time she would get dressed without tantrum behavior or any other form of refusal, she would earn a check. To get TV the next day, she would need five checks (i.e., perfect performance). If she wanted to argue about getting dressed it was going to cost her TV privileges the following day. In a three-month intervention period, how often do you think she lost TV? *Once!* Yes, I said once! You see, sometimes a contingency works so well you need use it only sparingly, and the problem behavior is "suppressed" for a long time.

What Should a Parent Do if the Child's Problem Behavior Returns to Its Previous Unacceptable Level?

The reassuring news is that if you remove the consequence and the behavior problem reappears, research definitely points to the efficacy of reinstating the punishment contingency. Reinstating the consequence will almost always result in an eventual return to low levels of the child's target problem behavior, as was achieved before.

In many of the clinical cases my behavioral specialists and I have been involved with, we intervene for a 3- to 6-month period. By the end of that period, if we have designed an effective strategy, the problem behavior has disappeared or certainly reduced in frequency, to a tolerable level. We terminate the case successfully, wish the family well, and move on to other families with challenging problems. However, it is not uncommon to get a call from the parent, sometimes several weeks after successfully terminating, with a phrase out of the movies: "It's back (meaning the problem behavior)!" In most cases, simply reinstating the previous plan works as it did before.

Let's suppose Jack's parents had decided that they would no longer "hold early bedtime over his head." If Jack promised that he would treat his sister with the respect he has learned to show her over the past 12 weeks, they would allow him his regular bedtime every night. Guess what. Although Jack promised to respect his sister, in a few weeks he is back to calling her the names on a daily basis. So much for promises! Jack realizes that this behavior no longer produces loss of regular bedtime. Now, Jack's parents are even more upset with him because in addition to being mean to his sister, he also does not keep promises. What are Jack's parents to do? (*Note to reader: this is often the reason why the parents claim the behavioral plan did not work. The child's problem behavior reappears when they drop the plan abruptly.*)

Luckily, Jack's parents don't panic and call 911. After taking a deep breath and recollecting themselves, Jack's parents redeploy the original plan, with early bedtime. Two check marks on a given day result in Jack going to bed a half-hour earlier. Three checks result in him going to bed one hour early. More than three checks, result in him going to bed right after supper. With this "heads-up" thinking, Jack's parents see a return to desirable interactions with family members.

If a behavior returns, the parent should simply reassess the problem and return the plan, in force, to retrieve the more acceptable level of behavior. Very often this return to the effective manner of dealing with the misbehavior is the key.

Myth # 3: Punishment Causes Problems for
a Child's Emotional Development

What Types of Problems Are Purported to Occur with the Use of Punishment?

Punishment is at the root of all evil, or at least at the root of emotional and behavioral difficulties a child exhibits, as some would contend. When a child misbehaves, you may have heard some people refer to the child's behavior as "acting out." You might have been dumbfounded since you saw no relationship between hitting the wall in anger and some acting performance on the part of the child. Acting out refers to an assumption that the child is acting out his internal conflict(s) through the misbehavior. This conflict is theorized to occur when the child's natural desires come in conflict with the dictates of the environment, A.K.A, parental consequences.

Further, such difficulties are theorized to extend past childhood, to affect the personality of the adult, unless unresolved conflicts created by punishment become resolved. People who have a variety of difficulties as adults are assumed to have been the recipients of great amounts of severe punishment as children. Proponents of this theory conduct the following research. Someone who is maladjusted as an adult is interviewed as to their being the victim of punishment. The person reports that his or her parents were strict. Being strict, usually invoking corporal or physical punishment, is equated (incorrectly) with punishment. Hence punishment is linked with whatever type of social mal-adjustment the individual exhibits.

If you have kept track of one of the central arguments of this book, my objection to these anecdotes is probably already clear to you. What definition was used for punishment? Yes, a procedural definition was probably invoked. One cannot ascertain that such a consequence effected successful changing of any misbehavior with these people during their childhood. But to these critics, paddling and punishment are synonymous. Hence these critics conclude punishment did occur. Further it is invoked as the causal factor in the person's current malaise.

If we by-pass the outcome-oriented definition issue for the minute, what is wrong with linking severe parental consequences to current or future social maladjustment? Because he got paddled, he is now the town alcoholic. This event, to the exclusion of all other events that were part of this child's upbringing, is deemed to be the responsible causal agent. How can anyone pointing to that event be absolutely certain that one caused the other? Why is such an explanation taken as fact by the professional community? Can you say Freud?

As you might have guessed by now, this certainty on the part of such proponents is rooted in psychoanalytic theory. Probably the most popularized maxim of this fictional account of the genesis of adult problem behavior is the often-cited scenario of punishment during toilet training. As the story goes, punishment during toilet training can be the causal factor in the genesis of all kinds of human frailties from anxiety disorders to personality quirks. According to Freud and many of his ardent followers, punishment during toddler toilet training produces a conflict. The conflict exists between the needs of the child to be uninhibited with respect to urges and the environment's requirement for certain proscribed behaviors. If adults would not impose any requirements on where elimination occurs, I guess Freud would say that intrapsychic conflict would not occur, at least with regards to that psychosexual stage. Of course Freud didn't speculate how many of these uninhibited children would become teenagers who would be perfectly comfortable having bowel movements in their pants. Perhaps that would not have been much of a social problem in Vienna in the early part of the 20th century. While this particular version of how punishment effects later behavior may be out of favor with regard to large scale popularity, its cousins (regarding early experiences as primary factors in adult behavior) are still alive and well in our culture.

How many times have you seen a movie called a psychological thriller that depicts a ruthless psychopath wrecking destruction in his/her wake. At some point in the movie, the movie viewer is given a glimpse of the psychopath's life as a child, relating some aspect of his or her upbringing to the development of this wretched personality. If only this child would not have been punished by his cold cruel mother while having sexual feelings for his older sister, when he was eight years old, he would not have grown up to become the Philadelphia Strangler. Unfortunately, it becomes difficult for the public to separate fiction in the movie from fact. This logic regarding the disastrous long-term effects of punishment pervades many professional and lay publics' explanation for a child's problem behaviors. The fictional anecdote below illustrates the nature of this logic.

Vera: Hey Margie, good to see you. How's everything? How's your son, Johnny? How is he doing in school? I know he has had a rough time in the past. Have things improved for him?

Margie: Oh, I think things are going to get much better. He is still having difficulties, but thanks to a wonderful book I am reading about disturbed children, I finally comprehend the reason for Johnny's difficulties.

Vera: That sounds great! You know my son, Harold, had problems in following teachers' directions. They would ask him to come inside from free play and he would be oppositional and disrespectful as well. I worked with the teacher on this. I told Harold he was to start following such teachers' directions. I gave the teachers permission to subtract free time from his upcoming recesses when he failed to come back to class upon command. Further, the teacher lets me know if he has called her names each day. If he calls the teacher names, I remove all his afternoon and evening privileges. He cannot go out with his friends that afternoon and loses all TV access that night. It gives him lots of time to think about how he will handle himself tomorrow. Since the first few incidents in the first 3 weeks of school the teacher is now reporting that Harold is much improved and has not lost any free time for the last 5 consecutive weeks. Why don't you consider something along those lines, it worked great for Harold.

Margie: Oh no, that is the wrong way according to this book I am reading. (*Note to reader: Proponents of the Dr. Do-nothing approach are not cognizant of real life results and data.*) In his book, *How to Handle Your Emotionally Sensitive Yet Gifted Child*, Dr. Do-nothing clearly explains that such punishment procedures make children resentful of authority. Further, that resentment builds over time so that they carry this resentment of authority figures to all aspects of their life. This can then lead to your child becoming an adult who does not trust other people, thus leading to an insecure and emotionally fragile existence.

Vera: You don't say? (with a look of bewilderment)

Margie: This is why my Johnny has such a difficult time in school with teachers. I unfortunately would put him in time-out when he would hit me, before I read this wonderful book. Even though he stopped hitting me when I used time-out consistently, unfortunately, Dr. Do-nothing believes that this parental response to hitting built up a lot of emotional turmoil inside of Johnny. You see, not being trained in these things, I had no way of knowing that I was causing him more harm than good. I was putting my need to have him respect me ahead of his need to explore his environment in a safe manner, free from inhibition. Punishing him with time-out shook the bond of trust and attachment he had with me. His misbehavior was a reflection of this lack of trust. So I had to stop using time-out consequences for his behavior to begin to rebuild our relationship. I now try to understand what he is going through as he struggles with these trust issues. It would be harmful to punish him for his struggles. (*Note to reader: The misbehavior is disregarded, because of this hypothesized "struggle."*) While it is true that he was suspended 5 times just this year because he was disrespectful to teachers, he is growing emotionally. Thanks to Dr. Do-nothing, I have learned that his rebellion is just a stage that he must go through before he achieves harmony with his environment. Then he will become a responsible young person. It is within him, I only hope I don't get in the way of his development.

Vera: Well that is interesting. (Thought to herself: *Boy I would burn that book if I were Margie.*) I hope everything goes better for you and Johnny. Maybe we can get together Wednesday afternoon for coffee.

Margie: I would love to, but I have another parent-teacher conference because Johnny told the principal that he would stay out on the jungle gym as long as he wanted to. I have to go straighten them out about the needs of this type of child: the emotionally sensitive yet intellectually gifted child. These people just don't know how to handle children like Johnny.

What is Wrong with this Contention?

Primarily that it is an unproven contention. Is there cause and effect research data to demonstrate that using a punishing consequence for a target problem behavior produces harmful effects to a child's development? Obviously not, since most of the information for this theory regarding the harmful effects of punishment is a post hoc inspection of childhood events, long after the fact. In addition, one looks for parental practices as the culprit of adult maladjustment, to the exclusion of all other phenomenon.

What would be reasonable scientific evidence that outcome-oriented punishment, while effective for the target behaviors, produces immediate deleterious short-term effects? Two findings should appear in studies. First, the punishing consequence would produce a change in the target behavior (i.e., outcome-oriented punishment). Second, a concurrent side effect to other behaviors or aspects of the child's life would result. In other words, only successful demonstrations of punishing consequences would qualify as the criteria for studying harmful side effects. I am sure that unsuccessful uses of consequences have disastrous effects, primarily where the target (mis)behavior is still rampant in the child's repertoire.

What Harm Would Such a Myth Cause?

If someone led us to believe that taking a flu shot for the flu is a dangerous intervention because it leads to insanity 3 months after ingestion, what would be the effect on public health if the public believed it? You can readily see what would happen. People would stop getting flu shots. It certainly would make many more people sicker with flu symptoms than need be, perhaps increasing the mortality rate from catching the flu. Of course, this unsupported contention regarding the relationship between the flu, getting a flu shot, and becoming mentally deranged would be quickly discounted as having no basis in scientific findings by the medical profession. However, unsupported contentions regarding causal variables of emotional problems people experience have never been brought to the fore for the same critical analysis by scientists.

What is wrong, and subsequently deleterious, with the contention that Johnny's mother makes (that use of consequences are what causes his problems at school)? Note that the focus of concern for her and Dr. Do-nothing is *not* the immediate behavioral effects of any strategy on his school behavior. As many of you would agree, the focus of concern should be on Johnny's problem behavior at school. Why would she not be concerned about his behavior at school? Perhaps because she has been *brain washed* into believing that there are bigger fish to fry. Unfortunately, his behavior at school, in desperate need of contingencies, never gets that intervention. And the effect on his subsequent behavior is one of non-effect. In fact, with professional suggestions such as removal of consequences for undesirable behaviors, what do you think happens with these children? The undesirable behaviors often become exacerbated in frequency, form, and intensity. You would think this would be a signal for some parents and professionals to reconsider, but unfortunately it often is not.

How can they get away with this? These advocates of non-consequence- based approaches will stipulate that their approach may not produce immediate gains to actual behavior. Rather, this " enlightened" method of handling the child's behavior takes a long time to sink in, and therefore one should not be discouraged when the problem behavior does not improve in the short-term. Of course to some of these experts, short-term can be years (or decades)!

If this reminds you of the fable about the emperor's new clothes, it should. If you get people to believe that anything that produces an immediate change in a child's behavior as a result of consequences is harmful, they will see a dressed individual when that person is actually naked. You might remark to yourself, "Certainly, they will see the obvious." However, when you show them someone who is naked, their remarks astound you. "Oh, she only looks like she is naked. This is an illusion. If you could see like I see, you would see she has beautiful clothes on." The analogy: You may think your child is doing better because his behavior is improving, but deep inside the "psyche," he is all screwed up (you have to take their word for that).

Concurrently, an intervention that is ineffective in the short run is a sign of good news, to them. This means that this child will be a markedly better adult 10 years from now, because he is obviously struggling with all this conflict. In other words, the opposite is true. These people will swear that they see clothes on someone who is nude. What is the upshot? Often, the clothes never arrive and many parents are duped into believing that the clothes were on their way. In truth, they never had much of a chance to arrive.

Let me state emphatically, children like Johnny, who engage in such behaviors are in desperate need. These children need to develop more emotionally responsible behaviors to the everyday demands from their environment. This behavioral development occurs when adults in the child's life provide consequences for both appropriate and undesirable behaviors. All the sophisticated theorizing in the world is not going to change Johnny's way of doing business if the social environment does not consequate unacceptable ways of responding. If Johnny's mother would take the advice of her friend, Johnny would learn that complying with the school rules and being respectful to school personnel produces dense and varied reinforcement. Concurrently, failing to do such would result in a less desirable set of circumstances. Children learn by what we do.

As a side note to the dialogue above, did you note that suspension from school was not an effective punisher of Johnny's oppositional behavior toward school rules? Let me pose some questions for you as food for thought. Why do you think that suspension from school did not decrease Johnny's behaviors? What do you think his mother does to him when he is suspended? What would her friend do if her son (Harold) were suspended? Does suspension function as a punisher for all children? What do you think must be in place if suspension from school is to effectively reduce the behavior of children like Johnny? Would it be better for schools to intervene in other ways when suspension does not function as a punisher? For more information on classroom contingency management, I would refer the reader to my book (Cipani, 2004) on the topic, *Classroom Management for All Teachers: 12 Plans for Evidence-based Practice.*

When You Punish Children for a Behavior, Don't They Become Upset?

How many children cry when they are put in time-out? My answer is many. Some children also throw tantrums, can be aggressive and so forth. These reactions can also occur for other punishing consequences, including the failure to earn points toward a sizable reinforcer. Not all children engage in such behaviors; some children have learned to accept these consequences. But a fair number of children do engage in crying and other forms of behavior indicative of discontent. This short-term emotional response does occur to the imposition of the consequence. Once the consequence is removed, and the child returns to previous stasis, such behaviors disappear.

If a punishment intervention produces such a short-term emotional response, is that a "bad thing?" Some professionals and parents apparently think so. Perhaps they believe that children should always be happy and in perfect harmony with their environment. I guess we should only find out that life isn't perfect when we turn 18.

Being upset when you receive a consequence for misbehavior is natural. No one is happy when they lose extra recess, TV privileges, or a promotion at work. If that weren't the case, police officers that hand out tickets would be one of the most popular groups of people in the community. They would be invited to all types of social events and be asked to bring their ticket books in case someone at the party needed a ticket. Upon receiving such, the recipient would thank the officer and inquire how she or he could receive another ticket.

Sarcasm aside, adults also often have short-term emotional responses to contingent punishing consequences. In this regard children are no different. Some children are unhappy about receiving a punishing consequence and express such in the form of crying. The first mistake is to assume this is anything more than a short-term phenomenon. The second mistake is to make this reaction to the consequence delivery the basis for why punishment is not desirable: Because he cries!

Are These Reactions to Punishment Tough for Many Parents to Handle?

Yes! Many parents struggle with this issue. They have been told that the side effects of punishment such as crying, pleading, tantrums and other emotional responses, are an indication of two undesirable phenomena. First, such reactions indicate that the consequences lack the ability to handle the child's behavior (wrong on the first count). Second, it is evidence that punishment is undesirable as a method of dealing with child behavior (wrong on second count). Hence, parents see their child cry upon the delivery of a punishing consequence and believe they are doing something wrong. They feel guilty and wish to apologize to someone for having to punish a child's behavior. Very often, parents utter the following infamous words, "Now Johnny, this hurts Mommy more than it hurts you when I have to put you in time-out." I have seen parents sit with their child while she or he is in time-out, explaining to the child how bad they feel because she or he is in time-out. One of my behavioral specialists reported to me that one of the mothers she was working with sat right next to her child and actually cried, with her child, when he was placed in time-out. How well do you think that time-out procedure worked for that family?

What is the Result of this Parental Guilt?

To avoid "provoking" the child's crying, some parents will infrequently consequate problem behaviors, particularly in a systematic fashion. Because of the lack of systematic consequences, these parents fail to address effectively the problem behavior in the first place. If a parent stops using time-out as a consequence, their child will obviously not cry (because she is not in time-out). This is true. However, what does this do for her problem behavior (i.e., hitting her sister)? Infrequent and inconsistent consequences are usually ineffective, hence their failure to control undesirable behavior.

If on the other hand, these parents are taught that providing consequences for unacceptable child behaviors is not only an effective way to manage such behaviors, but is justified, then they would feel less guilt. It is tough for almost all parents to see their kids cry. My mother had a great saying for that, "Better you cry now than I cry later!" Think about that. My mother was extremely astute, despite the fact she never completed high school (she grew up in the depression). I thank her everyday, and I am in her debt.

Is There Any Research Evidence Regarding Positive Short-term Emotional Effects?

Again we have probably all witnessed children responding in an unhappy manner to parent levied consequences. I do not deny that such phenomenon exists. I would contend that such a result in the beginning is not a bad thing. It is probably indicative of the consequence creating a condition that the child will wish to avoid in the future. Many children who experience time-out the first few times cry. I usually take that as a sign: If time-out is implemented consistently, it has a good shot at working.

Does outcome-oriented punishment produce undesired changes to other behaviors or aspects of the child's emotional development? With regard to children, there are just a few studies that have examined this experimentally (Lovaas & Simmons, 1969; Otto, 1976).

In his extensive nationally renowned work with children with autism, Dr. Ivar Lovaas at the University of California at Los Angeles in 1969 found that punishment procedures eradicated severe self-injury (Lovaas & Simmons, 1969). But he also noted that some of the children became more socially responsive to the adults. For example, John, an 8-year-old child with severe mental retardation, engaged in self-destructive behavior since the age of 2. He would take his fist to his head, producing contusions and bruising on his head. At the age of 7, after extensive attempts from John's parents to maintain him in their household, they had to place him in a state institution. When he was admitted to UCLA facilities, he had to be restrained continuously in order to prevent him from hurting himself.

While I know some of you may cringe at reading this, in order to produce a sufficient consequence for such self-destructive behaviors, a one-second shock was delivered when John attempted to injure himself. This obviously was under the close supervision of clinical staff at UCLA. The effect was immediate; no more attempts at self-injury. Compare this with the years of parental efforts that resulted in the failure to inhibit John's self-destructive behavior. Dr. Lovaas noted that in addition to his refrain from hurting himself, his whining behavior reduced noticeably. Another positive side effect of this treatment was that John was increasingly approaching the adults involved in his treatment. Funny, "psychological theory" would have predicted that he would avoid these adults at all cost because they were associated with punishment. Seemingly, the punisher produced positive benefits. Can you see why it is important to collect data instead of only speculating?

Unfortunately, as you can readily see, the research base regarding the emotional side effects of outcome-oriented punishment is not extensive. One cannot conclude unequivocally that positive side effects always occur. We just do not know enough at this stage of research. Further, because of the prohibition on studying punishment, it does not appear that we are on track to learn more about the side effects of outcome-oriented punishment to a child's emotional state. The overt and covert professional ban on such research has certainly contributed to such a lack of understanding, which is extremely unfortunate.

Does Aggression Beget Aggression?

Many critics of physical punishment state that such procedures model aggressive behavior on the part of the parent and therefore make it more likely that the children will acquire aggressive repertoires themselves. To provide a factual basis for such a contention, animal research conducted in the 1960s showed that animals exhibit aggressive behavior when they are shocked (Azrin, Hutchinson, & Hake, 1967; Ulrich & Azrin, 1962). If you teach a pigeon to peck a key to get food and then apply shock to the pigeon for the key peck, it will aggress against the cage or another bird. Further, the same aggressive behaviors occur when you simply remove food reinforcement as the consequence of key pecking (Azrin, Hutchinson, & Hake, 1966). In other words, presentation of a powerful consequence such as shock or the removal of positive reinforcement has the same side effect: emotionally undesirable responses (Azrin, Hutchinson, & Hake, 1966; 1967). Both the presentation of an aversive event as well as the removal of reinforcement were equally adept at developing this aggressive reaction.

Is this not evidence that bad things can happen with punishment? Not exactly. In these studies, such reactions to punishment were just allowed to occur, without any consequence. What if a consequence is delivered to the subsequent aggressive behavior (i.e., punish the aggressive behavior)? Can aggressive behaviors occurring as a result of the punisher be eliminated through punishment contingencies applied to such behaviors themselves? Obviously this is an important issue. If a procedure that solves one problem generates more problems, it certainly needs to be considered a risky venture when intervening. Failure to find a mechanism that lessens or eradicates the potential side effect of punishing consequences would certainly mitigate against its use.

In a study that examined that question, with three monkeys serving as involuntary participants, the monkeys were shocked every 30 seconds (Azrin, 1970). The shock was not contingent (dependent) on any behavior. This noncontingent aversive event produced the side effect of the monkeys biting a pneumatic tube inside their cage. Yes, monkeys get upset at being shocked! This tube automatically recorded each bite, thus providing an accurate measure of aggression. As long as the bites went unpunished, biting the tube following the receipt of shock was a given. However, once a sufficiently intense shock followed each bite on the tube, zero or near zero rates of biting the tube resulted for all three monkeys. Sure, the monkeys were still frustrated, but they found another way to deal with such frustration. Apparently, the type of emotional reaction to such an aversive event depends on the consequence of the reaction. If the monkeys could talk, they might have told the interviewer from CNN, "Boy, I am mad, but I am not going to take it out on that tube." What a paradox; shock purportedly elicits such aggressive behavior but when it is used as a contingency it also eliminates aggressive behavior as a reaction to frustrating events. Perhaps the method of handling inappropriate and undesirable reactions to consequences needs to be examined. I am not suggesting the method used in the study above, but an additional consequence does seem to be a possible fruitful approach.

What is Your Best Guess about Short-term Side Effects of Punishment?

I would venture to guess that positive side effects would occur if the change in the child's targeted behavior was fairly dramatic. For example, if you change the level of sibling aggression in a family, would that not have an effect on how the two siblings get along with each other? Further, with the increased positive relationship between the two siblings, the rate of their mom or dad intervening in a negative fashion would be less frequent. Do you suspect that the amount of positive attention and praise would also increase, given that more appropriate play between the two is now occurring?

In my clinical work, when a consequence is successful over a period of time in modifying a problem behavior, effects to other areas of functioning have usually been positive. The case below is an illustrative example.

The Case of: "I Grew to Love You."

It is always hard when young children are removed from their mother's home due to no fault of their own. Such was the case in one of my referrals for two sisters, ages 4 and 6, who were having extreme difficulty in their first foster placement after being detained by Child Protective Services (CPS). The foster mother, who had already raised her own children, did not know how to handle the defiance and oppositional behavior that occurred subsequent to their visits with their biological mother. The children's behavior, in particular the older one, made this foster mother raise concerns to the social worker within a month of placement.

These two girls visited their mother weekly at the CPS facility. While the girls would certainly enjoy the visit with their mother, leaving her was less than pleasant. Certainly in the beginning one would expect a great amount of emotion from these two girls. However, what was becoming a pattern was not solely an emotional response to a sad and depressing situation.

Althea, the older sister, would become oppositional, scream without provocation and engage in inappropriate verbal comments shortly after each scheduled visit with their mother. As soon as she would leave the room with her mother, she would become short, snippy and rude to the foster mother, Ms. Holly. I am sure Althea hated to leave and maybe this was her way of telling people that she wanted to go home with her mother. Althea would also attempt to enlist her sister, Maria, to help in the verbal defiance and oppositional attitude. She would attempt to make a pact with Maria for both of them to misbehave after the visit. Anything Ms. Holly would say would seem to provoke a negative defiant reaction from Althea. The first several visits were largely made up of a defiant response from the point they left the CPS office to the time they got home and beyond. Ms. Holly might ask Althea, "How was your visit with your mom," or "How did you like the toys in the room?" This would be met by some response along the following lines: "I don't have to talk to you. I don't like this place. Leave me alone." (Insert a defiant attitude with that verbal response.) The social worker spoke to both girls about their situation and how it is important to get along with Ms. Holly, because she is wanting to help both Althea and her sister. Further, Ms. Holly was having difficulty with the children regarding other behaviors at home as well. In other words this placement was not headed for calm waters.

These types of situations are heart breakers for everyone involved. When you see kids crying because they can no longer stay with their mother, we all cry. Why should children pay the price for an adult's mistakes and shortcomings? But alas, that is the case. However, my job is to make the short-term living arrangement more comfortable for everyone. Having the children bounce around from home to home, because of their behavior, is not good for them irrespective of the rotten turn their lives have taken. While I certainly felt sorry for them, it was very clear in my mind what needed to be done in the short-term. I had to make this arrangement workable for everyone, especially the foster mother.

One note needs to be made about this foster mother. She was one of the most kind and considerate parents I have met in my years of providing in home behavioral parent training for CPS. I felt that any child would be lucky to have her as a parent. If Althea and Maria could not be returned to their mother for reasons beyond their control, I saw a bright future for them here. With the cards they were dealt with in life, this would be making the best of that situation.

How should we deal with this defiant behavior coming from Althea? I am sure that most people would think that a consequence for such behavior is the last thing you want to do. Well it was the first thing I wanted to do. I developed a contingency plan to address the defiant behavior coming right out of the gate, so to speak, following Althea's visit with her mother. I did not want her to get started with verbal defiance even before they got in the car, which was often the case. I have learned that often, if you break the chain of behavior right at the start, you generate a positive momentum. This is what was needed in this situation. Therefore, if both girls were able to come out of the office and behave in a reasonable manner, without being oppositional or defiant, they would earn a trip to MacDonald's on the way home. The point at which Ms. Holly was to make the decision to award the MacDonald's trip was one block before reaching the fast food restaurant. Subsequent to leaving the CPS facility, Ms. Holly drove a route that would possibly end at MacDonald's. However, if any oppositional or defiant behavior occurred either at the CPS facility, or en route to MacDonald's, then the route was changed at that point, with a verbal explanation that they would not be going to MacDonald's because of the display of undesirable behavior. In other words, the punishing consequence for such behavior was the removal of the preferred event, MacDonald's. This plan resulted in an immediate change in Althea's behavior (as well as Maria!). How many times do you think Althea and Maria had to lose a trip to MacDonald's before she learned some self-control and respect for her new caretaker? How about not even once! It does not look like punishing consequences had an ill effect on their emotional level at that point. As a matter of fact, in my data gathering with Ms. Holly about the effectiveness of the plan, she indicated that both girls loved the trip to MacDonald's, and always looked forward to it. Fortunately in this particular situation, the threat of losing the trip eliminated the target undesirable behavior rapidly.

This was the good news. The bad news was that this plan generated a second problem. Althea would refuse to leave when she was told it was time to go. This secondary problem was handled successfully by the use of a timer to signal the end of the playtime on the playground and time to leave. Ms. Holly was instructed to inform Althea that it was about time to leave. She would also inform her that she was setting the timer for 5 minutes. When it rang it was time to go. Failure to leave the playground area immediately would result in the loss of the next trip to MacDonald's. The plan worked wonderfully. In short Althea seemed amenable to the use of contingencies in a very short period of time. Further it did not appear to be having an ill effect on either her or her sister. They were becoming more caring and loving toward their new caretaker, not less, as some one would predict. As Forrest Gump would say, they were as happy as two peas in a pod.

To handle tantrums occurring in the home a time-out procedure was selected. During the first 8 days of intervention with time-out, Althea went to time-out between 3 and zero times per day (actual data- 1,3,3,1,1,2,0,3). Maria had 4 time-outs across all 8 days. To make tantrum behavior even less "profitable" for either Althea or Maria, I instituted the "marble jar" plan. Each time either one went to time-out, a marble was dropped in the marble jar. If either one reached three marbles, she would go to bed early. With that additional contingency, neither girl went more than once to time-out in a given day. It was often the case that whenever I made a home visit both girls would greet me at the door and say, "I did not lose any marbles today/ yesterday, etc." Once the first marble was dropped, they clearly learned to demonstrate more self-control. The marble jar plan increased both girls' self-control. Increased self-control may have also been facilitated via some level of competition between the girls to be the one with the least number of marbles on a given day.

Compliance was also a problem in the beginning, and time-out was added as a consequence for noncompliance when needed. Overall, time-out combined with the marble contingency was very effective in getting both children (particularly Althea) to comply with instructions. Additionally, both girls became more adept at accepting a consequence, rather than escalating into more severe tantrum behaviors. Further, despite my role in the development and delivery of such consequences, both girls were usually excited to see me on my visits.

In summary, the problem behaviors delineated in the original assessment were no longer occurring at a level that could be considered problematic. What is also important is that both these children, in my humble opinion, grew to love their new mom. This was evidenced in many ways, from the way Althea beamed when she brought home a good note from school to the way she always looked for Ms. Holly's approval. I do believe that addressing their problem behaviors by using consequences aided not only with the remediation of these problems, but added a semblance of "family" to this newly comprised family unit. Althea and Maria seemed to be happy living with Ms. Holly, as well as continuing to spend a weekday afternoon with their biological mother.

Some people would have objected to the use of consequences for these children on the grounds that they have experienced considerable trauma in their lives (true), and that punishment can only add to that (totally untrue as is evident). I felt that consequences for these behaviors were the one clear justifiable thing to do. What do you suspect would have been the result if the girls continued to be disrespectful to their new caretaker and engage in tantrum behavior and noncompliance? Do you think that would have made them happy? Would it have made Ms. Holly happy? Would the girls have developed a love and respect for Ms. Holly? If your answer is, "Yes," to any or all of these questions, you probably also believe that pigs can fly, despite the incontrovertible evidence pointing to this absurdity!

- Why was Althea being so oppositional in the beginning? How was that changed with the behavioral plan?
- Why would it not have been a good idea to ask Ms. Holly to "ride out the storm?"
- Are the girls going to hold a grudge for the rest of their lives over Ms. Holly or myself?

Will Use of Punishing Consequences Result in Damage to a Parent-Child Relationship?

I believe that the above case demonstrates the fallacy of that supposition. The use of outcome-oriented punishment only enhanced the girls' relationship with their foster mother. Some "experts" claim that using punishment will cause your child to withdraw from you. You, as the source of punishment, will be avoided; hence your relationship with your child will be impaired. While there are no research studies that have addressed this potential side effect directly with children who are not handicapped, anecdotal evidence and information make this highly unlikely. I will plead my case.

While it is often the case that our children do not thank us for consequating their behaviors at the time of delivery, this is most often not indicative of anything other than a short-term response. Most of you would report that when this happens, sometime afterward, your child comes out of her "shell" and begins treating you in the same manner as before. Further, think back to when you were a child and teenager. I am sure you did the same to your parents when they presented consequences for your behavior. You may have thought to yourself: "Boy am I going to remember this for my entire life." Did you hold a grudge for your entire teenage life? Anecdotally, it does not appear that the use of punishment produces long-term avoidance of one's parents in the majority of people.

Almost all parents are the source of multiple reinforcers as well as punishment. With babies, parents feed them, take care of them, comfort them, and play with them. As they get older, parents care for them when they are sick, play with them, take them places, and hug them. Who takes them to soccer practice, little league, art club and band? Don't parents shower them with love and devote themselves to their children's welfare? If you select a few behaviors that produce punishing conse- quences, won't this be far outweighed by all the other positive time you spend with your child? I know that for many, many parents the answer is a resounding "Yes."

It is therefore inconceivable to me that a parent who applies a consequence to a teenager who comes home late one evening from curfew has done something that will do irreparable harm to a child's love for their parent. I do not have any scientific data to support my contention. But let me tell you that those who profess that punishment damages a parent-child relationship do not have any scientific evidence either. I do have evidence that using punishing consequences will effect the child's undesirable target behavior and not exacerbate it. On the other hand, not using consequences and relying on the child's natural tendency to discover that misbehav- iors are not in his or her long-term interests: where is that data?

Can a Parent be Primarily Associated with Punishment?

Highly unlikely unless all you do is deliver unpleasant events. For example, if you were a nurse in a hospital and the only time a pediatric patient saw you was when you delivered the "yucky," medicine, then I can see you becoming someone who gets patients hiding in the closets. But if you also provide other things such as comfort, reassurance, kind words, food, and honor various requests as the attending nurse, I don't think most patients would come out of the hospital despising the nurse.

When effective punishment occurs, the child learns to avoid the punishing event by doing what? By not doing the behavior that produces it! This can be illustrated in the following example. We all know that cars can get in accidents and cause injury. We have even seen car crashes and other severe accidents, possibly in person and/or on TV. How come we still get in the car and drive off each morning? Because of two things: the multitude of reinforcers available when you use the car and the ability of the driver to avoid getting in accidents by engaging in safe driving behaviors. Would it not be conceivable that more people would avoid driving if on a random basis their car's steering wheel would lock up (not as the result of what the individual did) and smash into something? But that describes a random application of an aversive event; Not a punishment contingency. If you were told that your car's steering wheel locks up whenever you turn it all the way to the right, you would learn to engage in driving responses that avoid performing that response. I am pretty certain that the majority of drivers would continue using their cars, but would never turn the wheel all the way to the right. One can avoid punishing events by not engaging in the behavior that produces such.

What Should Parents Keep in Mind When They Are Faced with Severe Reactions to Punishing Consequences?

We have a saying for parents when working with them on implementing a behavior plan: "When the going gets tough, stick to your guns." Do not judge what your child says when you impose the consequence as evidence that you have damaged your relationship. If you withhold outside privileges for the afternoon, your child will certainly not thank you because you have their long-term best interest at heart at that point. Your child will tell you it is unfair, that they cannot wait to be out of the house, and a host of other hurtful comments. I am sure you can fill in plenty of examples from your own experience. Further she or he may go to their room to sulk and discourage you from discourse for some period. This is not evidence that punishment contingencies are undesirable. Have patience. Things will turn around.

As I am sometimes on the scene when consequences are delivered, I have seen many parents just wilt when their child screams hateful remarks to them when in time-out. They turn to me and say, "He just said he hates me. Shouldn't I go in and reassure him that I still love him." My answer is always, "Yes, if you want him to make you feel like dirt every time he is put in time-out, go in right now and reassure him. By the way, have you noted that he only remarks that he hates you when you do something to him that he does not like. Why doesn't he say, 'I hate you!', when you are giving him a piece of pizza? However, if you want to wait to reassure him that you love him after he has finished his time-out and is busy playing, I think that would be a prudent choice on your part."

I know it is difficult to hear and see the things children do when they have to undergo consequences not to their liking. But take heart for the long run. Remember that you are also a source of reinforcement (love, support, and affection). This stalemate will not last. If you apply the consequence for a short period of time and then bring back the opportunity to earn afternoon privileges the next day, they will warm up to you again. You will be reassured that they still love you, but they also know there are consequences for behavior and will now respect you. The previous cold shoulder your child gave you when she or he lost outside time will fade away once she or he earns the privilege to go outside again, through acceptable behavior.

How Should a Parent Handle More Severe Reactions to Punishment?

Many children simply cry when placed in time-out or loss of a privilege is issued. After a few applications, they learn to accept the consequence and move on with their life. However, some children up the ante. I would contend that such reactions to consequences are learned from the parent's reaction to such behaviors. At any rate, when these severe reactions to punishment occur, they can pose a problem.

Some children can engage in a variety of behaviors that are intended to escape such situations. Screaming. kicking, yelling, profanity, and other undesirable behaviors are intended to teach you two lessons: (1) stop this unpleasant event right now and (2) don't even think about doing this again in the future. Of course, stopping the use of consequences because of the aggressive or defiant responses a child exhibits is not the right thing to do. But that is what many people do because they have been told that a child's discomfort is a sign that you are not being a sensitive parent. In these cases you are strongly advised to get technical assistance from a Board Certified Behavior Analyst or BCBA. You can go to *www.bacb.com* for a listing of these people. This situation may be beyond the scope of most parents' ability to handle alone.

Is it Possible to Teach Children to Accept Punishing Consequences?

How does one change a child's behavioral reaction to consequences? A didactic presentation of the benefits of accepting consequences, while certainly appealing, is most often ineffective with many children. We would all like to believe that telling the child he should not kick the plants over on the way to time-out should be sufficient. However, it is often ineffective. The child only knows that the more havoc he creates, the more perturbed his parent seems to get. The following case presents a method to teach a child how to accept consequences.

The Case of: "So You Won't Take a Time-out."

I was involved in a case of a 10-year-old child who was restrained daily by his mother. The restraint was typically around the mother's delivery of time-out, which was a consequence for aggressive behavior and attempts to destroy property in the home. Each day he would engage in aggressive behavior toward someone in the house or would throw some object against something. Each time he would behave in this manner, his mother would send him to time-out. Each time he was sent to time-out, he would fight back. Each time he would fight back she would restrain him until his time-out period was up. This was one tough lady, but unfortunately her persistence was not paying off. Her son did not appear to be profiting from the time-out consequence, as measured by lesser occurrences of aggression and property destruction. Further, the ruckus surrounding the time-out consequence did not appear to be improving. Each time-out resulted in a restraint from his mother. Many children his age require time-outs. But very few fight their parent (like he did) when it is time to go. What could I do to teach him to accept time-outs?

Then it hit me. How about a consequence for being restrained (in other words punish his unacceptable reaction to the time-out)? If he had to be restrained because of his oppositional behavior, then the consequence of that should be more than simply tiring his mother out. He apparently did not seem to mind the tussle. The following additional "back-up" contingency was invoked for any instances where a time-out had to be enforced through a parental restraint: he would go to bed an hour early. If he accepted his time-out, he could have multiple time-outs and nothing more would occur. However, fighting the time-out implementation and thereby requiring a restraint would result in the back-up contingency- loss of a later bedtime.

The results were immediate. No restraints were required after the first few days. We then attacked the frequency of the target behaviors in the same manner, thus bringing the level of such behaviors to a low rate (eventually only one- two per day). This strategy has proven successful with many other children since this case. It is imperative that children learn that these reactions to punishment will only bring more unpleasant consequences, and not their escape or avoidance of consequences for target inappropriate behavior.

- Was the restraining consequence effective in reducing the child's aggressive behavior?
- What usually happens when children protest (i.e., through their behavior) going to time-out? Does this possibly explain why time-out is ineffective in such cases?

Are Some Parents Just Not Able to Effectively Handle Their Child's Severe Reactions to Punishment?

Absolutely. I believe time-out procedures are very effective as an immediate consequence for children under the age of ten or eleven. However, I have learned over 2 decades that some parents are not capable, physically and/or emotionally, to place their children in time-out and keep them there until the crying and other behaviors stop for some period of time. In these situations, I may find it necessary to just restrict the time-out to a set period of time (e.g., 2 minutes), irrespective of what the child is doing at the end. It is not because I deem this to be a more effective approach for the child than a response contingent release (to be discussed later in this book). It is because I believe this approach has a greater likelihood of being carried out by the particular parent. In other cases, I do not even prescribe time-out because of my sense of the inability of the particular parent to effect it immediately and/or handle the child's behavior while in time-out.

It is important for a parent to come to grips with the saying, "Know thyself." Will you deliver the intended consequence? What will you do if your child refuses to go to time-out? If you sense that you may not be able to effect the plan you have designed, it might require that you develop an alternate plan. This is particularly relevant around the child's reactions to the delivery of the consequence. Of course, if your child objects to virtually any loss of events, you may need to start somewhere, possibly with the help of a board certified behavior analyst. On the spot coaching and help may be what you need to teach you how to deliver on your warnings.

In some situations, with two parent households, I use the "wait till Daddy comes home," strategy. On occasion, one parent has an inability to effect consequences, whereas the other parent is currently capable of presenting consequences to the child without much of a severe reaction. In these circumstances, when both parents agree, the parent with less influence is backed up by the parent with greater control over the child's response.

This strategy has been particularly effective in some families where the child "walks all over" one of the parents (more often his/her mother, but not always). The parent who does not have control, gains control, by being "backed up" by the parent who has better control. Further, such a transfer of behavioral control occurs without the mother having to physically intervene. Again, I would recommend that a family consider getting consultation from a behavior analyst before implementing such a strategy.

Does the Use of Punishment Cause Long-term Emotional Consequences that Impair the Individual When She or He Becomes an Adult?

Can punishment of child behavior cause an individual to grow up and become an alcoholic? Clinically depressed? What about a mass murder? Well, Ted Bundy probably was punished when he was a child and look what happened. There it is: proof positive that parents who use punishment will probably have a son like Ted Bundy. If you are punishing your daughter, she will probably grow up to be a female Ted Bundy.

While many people see how ludicrous this link is, there are continuing efforts to link childhood events to adult maladies. Psychologists, sociologists, and forensic researchers flock to prisons, juvenile halls, psychiatric hospitals, and other settings and try to find childhood experiences that some or many of the inmates or patients have had. Once again, such correlation research does not allow one to conclude cause and effect. However, there is an additional problem with this type of research.

Suppose a researcher finds that a group of prison inmates is twice as likely to have been punished with a paddle in comparison to a group of non-prison subjects. Does that prove that paddling causes delinquency? Suppose the number of people in prison who have been paddled is 25%. This rate turns out to be twice that in the general population, let us say 12.5%. However, even with that difference (assume that it is statistically significant), what do we know about most of the people (75%) in the prison group? They were not paddled. If paddling causes delinquency, would there not be a greater link between the two? How do you explain that 75% of the prisoners were not paddled as children? Furthermore, how do you explain that 12.5% of the people who were paddled, in the non-prison population, do not commit offenses?

Why is such correlation research inadequate for determining whether punishment produces long-term effects on adult development? The previous point I made regarding the inherent inability of correlation studies to allow for cause and effect analysis is still at the heart of the matter. Here again is the argument I pose. Suppose we see that the use of some punisher (e.g., time-out) is linked with higher rates of misbehavior in children. What this means is that children who have high rates of misbehavior, however defined, also experience more time-outs. On the other hand, children with low rates of misbehavior have lower levels of time-out. If such a study existed, its authors might conclude (erroneously) that there is a link between time-out and misbehavior.

Why does such a finding not allow one to conclude that heavier use of time-out causes children to engage in greater amounts of misbehavior? Turn the statement around. Greater rates of misbehavior cause greater use of time-out. Can that make sense? Linking two variables together does not give the direction of the causal arrow.

The biggest predictor of problems in adulthood in my opinion, is the inability to develop appropriate social behaviors as a child. With what we know from countless studies in behavior analysis, children who do not have such behaviors can acquire them, through contingencies and skill training. I would say that the presence of outcome-oriented punishment, along with reinforcement and skill training, are conditions that would make such human frailties less likely, although this is just my belief (i.e., no data to support such).

Myth # 4: Punishment Is Not as Effective as Reinforcement

Isn't it Common Knowledge that Reinforcement Works Better than Punishment?

You probably hear this often. "Punishment may work, but it is not as effective as a reward system. It is better to catch children when they are good and not to point out their behavior when they are bad." It is said so often that it is taken as fact. Where is the evidence that such a position is true?

There are many studies attesting to the efficacy of reinforcement procedures for a variety of child problem behaviors. One can certainly conclude that reinforcement procedures are effective. There are also many studies attesting to the efficacy of punishment procedures for a variety of child problem behaviors. Again, one can conclude that punishment contingencies are effective. Both sets of studies simply demonstrate that certain contingencies work for certain problems in certain contexts. What about a study that makes a comparison between reinforcement and punishment?

Which would be more effective, giving points to students for following the rules of the class or removing points for not following the rules? Which would the students prefer, the reward or response-cost procedure? A research study examined these questions during a math period in an elementary special education class (Iwata & Bailey, 1974). In the reward condition, the 40-minute math class was divided into ten intervals. For each interval during which the student obeyed the rules, she or he earned a token, with a maximum of ten tokens. Each student had to have at least six tokens in order to earn a snack. There was also a bonus day, with special reinforcers available for the 3 or 4 students who earned the most tokens up to that time. In contrast, the response-cost condition involved all students starting out with ten tokens. Each time a student broke a class rule, she or he would lose a token.

Which procedure was better for changing the level of rule violations? During the baseline condition, with no consequence for following or not following the rules, the rate of rule violations was 9% for the two groups of students. The rates of rule violation dropped to below 1% for both groups. Additionally, with the implementation of consequences, either reward or response cost, both procedures resulted eventually in a doubling of academic output. Off task behavior also dropped from baseline levels as well.

Did the students prefer the reward approach or the response-cost approach? In the last experimental condition of the study, the students could choose which of the approaches they wanted to be on each day. Four students consistently chose the reward, 5 chose the response-cost, and the remaining 6 subjects switched their choice at least once.

Further, the teachers' use of social disapproval remained about the same for both conditions. This is important to note because the disapproval rate of the teacher was not directly targeted. What can one conclude from these results? When powerful consequences are at work, there is no need for frequent negative comments to desist in some behavior. The consequence does its job!

In the above study, no significant difference was found between reward and response-cost contingencies. Note that the reinforcer available was the same for both groups; snack plus a surprise day. It apparently did not matter whether students earned points for following rules or lost points for not following rules, performance in both conditions was high. Reward was not better than response cost. This is the exact opposite of a myth perpetrated by many people who are unfamiliar with such research findings, as a personal story below illustrates.

I was hired to provide four sessions of training to school personnel, consisting primarily of school psychologists, special education personnel, and some school site administrators. In the early part of the first morning, one of the participants raised her hand and indicated that she learned that positives and rewards are more *effective* than taking away points for target misbehavior. She further claimed that there was a lot of research to bolster that fact. I inquired where this research could be found, and she said that this was something that a professor in her teacher-training program had said. I could not find tons of studies, nor could she, but here are some studies I did find.

Getting results faster. Can the use of punishing consequences, in conjunction with the removal of reinforcement, speed up the process of reducing a behavior? If such were the case, it would certainly provide a justification for the initial use of a punisher.

B. F. Skinner (1938) conducted a study with rats that addressed the efficacy of using punishment in addition to removal of reinforcement. Two groups of rats were trained to press a bar to get food pellets; bar pressing behavior was maintained on an intermittent schedule of reinforcement. Not every bar press resulted in a food pellet. Bar pressing became a frequent response under control of the food reinforcer for both groups.

In the test condition, one group of rats underwent an extinction process, which is the removal of food reinforcement. Each bar press did not result in food. The electronic machinery is very adept at insuring that bar presses no longer produce food (unlike humans who make some to frequent mistakes, even after verbally committing to extinction). The second group also received no food for bar pressing, but in addition each bar press resulted in the delivery of a punishing stimulus (you can guess what that was by now). What were the results? Combining a shock consequence with extinction produced faster and greater response reduction when both consequences were in effect. Seems like two is really better than one.

Reprimands are needed. A study sought to answer the question of relative effectiveness of reprimands versus and all positive approach (Pfiffner & O'Leary, 1987). Students from first, second, and third grades, attending a remedial summer program participated in this study. All students were reported by the regular school teacher to be functioning below grade level in math and/or reading. Six of the 8 students were also reported to have behavior problems, as measured by an often-used child behavioral rating scale, filled out by teacher interview.

Would a discipline program that revolves around all positive procedures be as effective as one that includes positive procedures plus reprimands for off task behavior? The management system the teacher implemented in the all positive approach included the following: verbal praise, public posting of completed work, and earning of stars each hour for good behavior and engaging in academic work. The stars were traded in for all types of activities and prizes on the reward menu. In the combined approach, all the positive procedures were used, but negative reprimands for off task behavior were also implemented.

In order to determine the effectiveness of the all-positive approach versus the combined approach, several measures of student performance and behavior were taken throughout the study. The rate of accuracy of daily assigned math problems was collected for each student in the study. Additionally, trained observers also measured the daily rate of on-task behavior.

The results revealed that the combined approach was superior to the all-positive approach for on-task behavior. Using only the all-positive approach, the mean on-task rate across all students was 56%. The range of on-task behavior during this condition showed great variability. The worst performing student's average on-task rate was 36%, while the highest performing student's average rate was 67%. During the combination, the average rate of on-task behavior across all eight students was now 80%. The worst performing student in this condition had a mean rate of 72%, higher than what was obtained in the all-positive condition for the best student. This study certainly seems to support a contention that adding consequences for off-task behavior in the form of reprimands improves what is achieved merely through the use of praise and tangible reinforcers.

Is the Intent of De-emphasizing the Efficacy of Punishment Procedures to Enhance more Positive Approaches for Dealing with Problem Behavior?

I am not sure what is meant by positive approaches, in terms of effectiveness. Something can look positive, but be completely ineffective. A car can be bright, shiny and look great, but sputter when driven over 30 miles per hour. What is an example of this with respect to child behavior and parenting? A hypothetical Dr. Feel Good has written in her book that the best parenting approach to dealing with a child's misbehavior at school is to discuss with the child, what their feelings and thoughts are regarding their behavior and its impact on the teacher's feelings. After such a discussion, the parent should "reach out" to their child and tell her them that they trust him or her to make the wise choice. Dr. Feel Good explains that a failure to trust your child to make good choices in life will upset the homeostatic relationship that may exist, and your child will resent such lack of trust later in life. Sound good? What parent would not like to be able to engage in such a positive approach to deal with presenting school behavior problems. While it looks great as a parenting strategy, does it effect the child's rate of misbehaviors at school?

If you have watched TV sitcoms over the last 20 years, you are lead to believe that this approach is the solution to all family problems. Open communication of feelings and dialogue between parents and their children are the sole requisites for parents. On TV, it looks so appealing and effective! After such a dialogue, which ends in tears of love and joy from everyone, the child goes back to school, having gained perspective on her misdeeds, and becomes a straight A student. And all within 30 minutes! Everyone would agree that such a manner of parenting would be preferable.

While that certainly is appealing, suppose discussions with children about their behavior do not lead to positive changes in their behavior at school. Some children keep engaging in such misbehaviors at school. As the unacceptable behaviors become more frequent and severe, the result of continued problems lead to greater disciplinary action on the part of the school. Again while this approach may appear to be the "humane" way of dealing with such problems, it unfortunately terminates in these children being expelled from school. I cannot view the repeated use of pleasant but ineffective parenting methods as a constructive method for dealing with child misbehavior. In my view, such a technique should be labeled, "well-meaning, but disastrous." If you have to choose, would you choose looking positive or being effective?

Now that I have clarified that point, back to the original question. If you prohibit the use of punishment procedures, would it naturally increase the use of positive reinforcement procedures? It seems to reason, if you remove one set of alternatives to dealing with behavior, the consumers of child discipline strategies must select another. Therefore if people are told that punishment does not work as well as reinforcement, wouldn't that force them to select only positive reinforcement approaches? Yes, I guess it might, possibly. Nevertheless, I have two concerns.

First, the field of applied behavior analysis, which has been distinguished by its reliance on empirically validated approaches, would have to undergo a philosophical transformation. It would have to become just another approach that promotes dogma in the face of contrasting evidence. This would not sit well with many behavior analysts. These people consider themselves to be scientists who apply research findings to their work with people. To advocate that approaches to human behavior be based on appeal rather than findings would (and should) be heresy.

I believe it is perfectly all right to state one's preference. I prefer to use reinforcement procedures that also entail withdrawal of reinforcement for target behavior problems. But I do not claim that other procedures that have an empirical basis are not effective or are less effective.

If you prefer to address problem behaviors via the use of positive reinforcement procedures, and are adroit and effective at doing such, then all power to you. But the operative requirement is success in changing relevant child behaviors. It is unacceptable when important child behaviors do not change, irrespective of what intervention is applied.

The second concern regarding restricting use of certain punishers is that the void may be filled by other procedures, such as an over reliance on medication to alter problem behavior. Evidence of this possibility can be found in what has transpired over time when punishment has been restricted in certain government agencies that regulate human service fields. In fields such as developmental disabilities, that use behavior analysis, certain "aversive" procedures are prohibited while reinforcement-based procedures are encouraged. Therefore, the contention was that restricting certain aversive techniques in institutional settings would naturally strengthen the use of reinforcement procedures. In a 1979 study, results showed that 50% of the patients in institutional settings for persons who have mental disabilities or mental retardation are on medication for behaviors (Aman & Singh, 1979). I would venture a guess that this finding is still relevant for today. Has the restriction of punishers in these institutions given rise to a greater reliance on reinforcement or medication to attempt to control certain problem behaviors? The answer seems obvious. Perhaps I can shed light on how this happens.

Got Meds?

I worked at two institutions for persons who are developmentally disabled in Wisconsin between 1979-1981, fresh out of graduate school. I was responsible for designing and writing behavioral plans for one residential unit, comprised of adolescents and young adults. The Wisconsin statutes regulating how I was to proceed in helping such individuals called for review of my written behavioral plans. I do not want to spend time detailing the entire statute so I will cut to the chase. If certain consequences were used, it merely required that my immediate supervisor review them. The "turn around time" was minimal at this level, perhaps 2-4 days. If other, more intrusive, consequences were to be used, then the supervisor and the institution's human rights committee would have to review the proposed plan. Of course if they wanted something changed, it was sent back to me for redesign and resubmission through the whole process. As you can see the length of the process has been expanded by an exponent. I do not want to give the impression that every resident I dealt with required this lengthy review. Many of the plans were exclusive of consequences that required such review. However, every so often, did I have a client with a problem! In some such cases, the only recourse I could see at that time was that reinforcement would have to be combined with some aversive consequence.

Contingent on successfully surviving that process, the written plans then had to go to a committee in Madison, Wisconsin for review. We are generally talking weeks, possibly over a month, before getting an answer. What was happening while all this review takes place? Back on the home front, staff persons who had to deal with such unacceptable and/or dangerous behaviors would look for someone to provide them with help. On my unit, as in others, we would convene meetings to determine what could be done. They would turn to me, and inquire, "Dr. Cipani, what can you offer us as a suggestion for when John Doe hits himself?" My reply was, "Well, I will have to collect data and then write a plan and then submit it to the process." They would politely reply, "OK, we will certainly hold our breath and wait for that." They would then turn to the institution's physician in attendance (or his/her substitute, the nurse) and make the same inquiry. Low and behold, this person would reply, "Well I can prescribe _____ for such a behavior and see if that works."

Hold on here! Let us play that back in slow motion. If the staff of the facility wanted behavioral plans, they had to wait some moderate to lengthy period of time for approval. However, if they were willing to go the medication route, they would get an immediate response. My thought at the time was, "Why is it I have to get everyone's permission to do something, and Dr. So and So consults himself or herself and then writes a prescription." If you were in the staff's shoes, whom would you turn to in a pinch. Not me! I have a "sometime in February" answer for you. Dr. So and So can help you right away. Does restricting some forms of punishment lead to greater use of positive reinforcement? I'll let you be the judge, but I do not consider medication a contingent positive reinforcer.

- What's wrong with this picture?
- What can be done to make social interventions more prominent as a means to change child behavior?

What Has Happened to Discipline in the Schools? Is There a Greater Reliance On and Use of Positive Reinforcement Procedures?

If the above example does not ring a bell, perhaps this one will. Where else is this reliance on nonsocial interventions taking place? How many times have we heard that the use of medication for school aged children is on a significant rise? Take this additional piece of information into account. Many school administrators and teachers report they have lost many of the discipline procedures involving consequences for problem behavior that were used decades ago. As the use of certain disciplinary consequences has decreased over time, has the use of positive reinforcement procedures increased? I don't think so. What apparently has filled the void created by prohibiting certain disciplinary tactics is more frequent contact with psychiatrists and pediatricians.

The field of applied behavior analysis has proven substantially, numerous times over, that reinforcement systems increase desirable behavior in children in classrooms (Cipani, 2004). I can't fathom how this is even a debatable point. However, such reinforcement approaches are not used often for children having behavior problems at school. Instead, a more frequent approach is for school personnel to suggest to the parent that she get a doctor to prescribe medication. I have had a couple of parents over the years tell me that such was a condition for the child's return to school from expulsion. In other words, the parent was told, "We will let Jose back to school if you agree to have him see a physician for medication for his behavior."

Why Can't Reinforcement Procedures be Used Instead of (or in Supplement to) Medication for Behavior Problems in School?

Nothing physically prevents it. In some cases with school behavior problems, I have used behavioral contingencies in conjunction with medication, and in other cases, I have used behavioral contingencies exclusively. It can be done. What prevents more widespread use of behavioral contingencies in conjunction with medication? Consider the following argument.

Medication, once prescribed by a physician, does not require any special skills on the part of the adult. One merely directs the child to open his or her mouth and insert the pill or liquid. But such cannot be said for behavioral consequences. Therein lies the answer.

I believe a greater use of behavioral contingencies in classrooms would solve many of the problem behaviors that teachers face today (Cipani. 2004). While I would like to see greater use of reinforcement procedures to increase appropriate behavior and academic engagement in materials, such is often not the case. What few consequences for misbehavior school personnel have at their disposal, they rely on frequently, (i.e., calling parents, detention, principal's office, suspension, and expulsion). However, a concomitant use of powerful reinforcement consequences for on-task behavior is typically not deployed with these strategies. Why?

Many university teacher-training programs, and their associated faculty, have a disdain (and lack of skill) for behavior analysis procedures. Hence, their consumers/students do not receive adequate instruction on such. If one does not receive training during professional preparation on such a technology, one would expect very few, if any graduates, to be capable of effectively using behavioral contingencies? Therefore, such future teachers ability to implement a behavioral plan based on reinforcement and punishment operations is handicapped in numerous cases, which brings me back to the original question. Can reinforcement be used in conjunction with medication? Yes, if the personnel have the capability to design and enact an effective plan. However, if such behavior analysis skills do not exist, what alternative becomes very probable when the behavior of the child is unmanageable, in spite of all the detentions and visits to the principal's office. Yes, you got it, medication. How to improve this situation? Only skill training in behavior analysis for *all* future teachers would have the desired effect.

Isn't it Common Knowledge that Punishment Does Not Teach a Child a New Behavior?

Punishment, or reinforcement for that matter, does not teach new behaviors. Punishment, like reinforcement, only alters a person's motivation to engage, or not engage, in a behavior that is already in the child's current repertoire. I often use this example to illustrate this point to students in my class. I ask them, "Who would be willing to earn a trip to Hawaii, all expenses paid for one week, for performing a behavior that would take no more than 30 minutes? It is not something that is illegal or would go against anyone's moral standards." Of course they all raise their hand. I then inquire, "Would you all say that you are sufficiently motivated to respond to my challenge?" Again they all eagerly raise their hand. I then say, "OK, let me give you a test of 10 problems in the content area of integral calculus (please assume that students in the class may only have familiarity with basic Algebra). You have 30 minutes to complete this test without referring to anyone or anything and if you score a perfect 100% you earn the trip."

While many students report they would try, all realize that they would probably not be successful. A free trip to Hawaii would certainly get them to perform a behavior that is in their repertoire, but it does not have such evocative effects when the individual cannot perform the behavior. What is needed in such a case is good solid instruction, along with reinforcement contingencies. Merely changing someone's motivation to perform a behavior does not alter its probability if the probability is null to start with. If someone were not capable of performing the target behavior, strengthening the reinforcer and/or punishing contingencies would not be fruitful. Reinforcement and punishment only makes behaviors currently in the repertoire more, or less, probable. Neither operation, in isolation, develops new repertoires.

Teaching Children How to Peacefully Co-exist with Pets

I am not suggesting that one should always approach a problem behavior with the intent to use a punishing consequence only. Far from it! That is not the first thing that comes to my mind when I am faced with certain problem behaviors. Here is a case in point. We have worked with several young elementary aged children whom I term: *animal destroyers*. For whatever reason, these children abuse animals. Some children have broken the legs of cats, grabbed dogs by their ears, or engaged in other similar abuse.

In some cases, prior to our involvement, these children have received individual psychotherapy. Such therapy was provided to find out why the child was hurting an animal, and what in their psyche could lead to such an exhibition of violence. Individual therapy is based on the premise that the child needs to gain insight into his internal conflicts. When individual therapy only resulted in continued aggression to animals, in addition to other behavioral problems, we would get the referral for behavioral management. I'll leave it to you to speculate how much insight these children gained up to the point when we initiated skill training and contingencies.

We have found it essential in these cases, especially with young children, to use a double pronged approach: Teach these children how to play with animals safely and punish any behavior that involves inappropriate contact quickly. For the former, we often start with getting the child to engage in hugging and petting stuffed animals, under close supervision. We show them how to pet the animal and then ask that they rehearse the demonstrated behaviors under our guidance. Our basic instructional procedure is to: (1) tell the child what to do, (2) show the child how to do it, (3) have the child rehearse the behavior we just modeled for them, and (4) give the child feedback on their performance.

Immediate correction of incorrect imitations of our modeled behavioral response is given in the beginning. Subsequent to the first few corrections, a mild punishment contingency is put into effect. Any inappropriate contact results in removal of the stuffed animal for a short period of time. Following this, we present continued practice on stroking the animal instead of choking it, hurling it across the room, or whatever other violent behavior may be the child's modus operandi with real animals.

Once the child learns to pet and play with the stuffed animal over two to three sessions, we then bring in the real animal. Under close supervision, the child is prompted to engage in the same acceptable loving behaviors. It is important to restrict the child's access to real animals as much as possible at times other than the training sessions in the beginning. Once the parent and we feel comfortable with their child's demeanor toward the animal, we provide greater access.

During this training, if the undesirable behavior toward the pet occurs, we immediately remove the child from the animal and place him or her in a time-out. Additionally, depending on the age of the child, we may also have a 1- to 2-day restriction from contact with the family pet for that child. After several sessions of appropriate supervised contact we then let the child have full access with this caveat: even attempt to be "mean" to the animal and you will pay the price. We have seen several children with this problem grow to have appropriate relationships with their animals and really appreciate their pets as animals with feelings. But it takes skill training and contingencies. Simply scolding the child, as a strategy to deal with animal abuse, in our experience, does not appear to be effective in the long run.

- Why was it essential to begin training with stuffed animals instead of real pets?
- What was the consequence for undesirable behavior toward a pet? Why do you think this was not carried out prior to my intervention?
- What is your theory about why some children engage in hurtful and dangerous behavior with their pets?

Does That Mean That Consequences are Irrelevant When Teaching Children Something New?

Quite the contrary. Make no mistake! Both skill training and consequences are needed when teaching a new behavior. As I pointed out above, consequences will not build in a behavior that is nonexistent. In order for consequences to work the behavior must already be in the child's repertoire. For example, in the animal laboratory, teaching procedures, called shaping, are used to teach the rat to press the bar or the pigeon to peck the key. You cannot simply place the animal in the cage and wait for him or her to bar press and then reinforce. Believe me, you would grow old waiting and the animal would probably starve. But once the animal is taught to press the bar (i.e., happens at some minimal rate), such behaviors will not become frequent without consequences.

Let us say that you see a need to teach your son how to play cooperatively with his older sister. When they are on the swing in the backyard, he has resorted to throwing her off, pushing her off, and grabbing her hair. All these unacceptable behaviors are actually very adaptive at getting the desired result. It is funny that many professionals in the field call these behaviors, maladaptive. They ought to see how useful they are in those situations in which someone is occupying the same space as you desire.

But let us get back to the issue at hand. One day you provide repeated practice at getting the children to take turns with the swing, using a strategy comparable to what was described earlier in this book's introduction with the children at Head Start. Toward the end of the day, they both seem to understand that they should come to you, and you designate, via an oven timer, who goes on the swing first, for how long, and so forth. You are smart not to let the same child go first each time but rather you alternate. You feel success, and you are proud of your children and yourself. Finally, peace will come to your home when the children are out playing.

This idyllic lifestyle will persist only for so long. When one of them engages in the previous adaptive behavior such as pushing, what are you prepared to do? Just give them a lecture about how they are to get along with each other? That would probably not be fruitful. On the other hand, if you consequate such behavior, with loss of access to the swing for some time, you have now made such behavior maladaptive and less likely. Skill training will have a greater effect when it is backed up with congruent consequences. Believe me, this applies even to adults.

If you teach your child that pushing someone off the swing is inappropriate, by teaching him how to wait his turn, then you must back that up with consequences. When he waits, he gets to enjoy the swing. When he does not wait, he loses access to the swing. Now which behavior is adaptive? Which is maladaptive? Skill training and consequences- the only way to fly!

Are There Any Studies That Have Used a Skill Training Approach with Consequences?

If you go out shopping on a regular basis, you probably have been horrified by what you saw some children exhibit while there with their parents. In the 1970s, the Family Training Program, under the Department of Human Development and Family Life at the University of Kansas, was available to parents to help them deal with child problems at home and school (Barnard, Christopherson, & Wolf, 1977). These researchers verified the need for child behavior management during shopping trips by interviewing store managers and mothers. The objective of a child behavior management training package would be to decrease the following two inappropriate child behaviors during shopping trips. First, the child should not be far from the parent and shopping cart. This was defined as being further than arms reach from the cart. Second, the child should not handle or disturb any of the products on the shelves or floor area without authorization. An independent observer who accompanied each mother recorded how frequently such target behaviors occurred.

To teach each child, appropriate behaviors were described and modeled by the researchers and the parent. The child was given an opportunity to practice such behaviors. Such skill training and verbal explanation of the types of behaviors desired is an essential component of the management effort. However, when only skill training is provided, in the absence of consequences implemented during the real-life condition, change in child behavior may not be realized.

The intervention also consisted of a reinforcement plan for appropriate shopping behaviors as well as a response cost for target behaviors. Each of the three participant mothers was taught how to reward appropriate behavior. They were taught to provide points, about two to three times per aisle, for appropriate behavior as well as how to remove points for engaging in either of the undesirable target behaviors (i.e., the response cost component). The balance of the points was combined with other points earned for behavior at home. The child exchanged points for items and privileges in the home.

The three boys who were the subjects of the study (ages 6, 6, and 5) all improved their shopping behaviors tremendously. As an example, Barney was away from his mother and the cart 49% of the time prior to the behavioral plan being implemented. When his mother reinforced proximal behavior and punished leaving the immediate area, his rate of being away from the cart dropped to 5%. Similar effects were observed for the other children and for product disturbance as well.

As you might guess, each mother rated her child's behavior as markedly improved subsequent to using the behavior plan. For example, during baseline, Barney's mother rated his behavior during three of the five shopping trips as poor. In contrast, Barney received an excellent or satisfactory rating from his mother on 15 of the 18 visits following implementation. Only three of these visits were rated as poor. Complaints about the child's behavior also decreased.

But there are some additional important findings of this study. Audiotapes of Barney's shopping trips were collected and scored by individual judges to determine if the use of the intervention package effected parent-child interactions. The percentage of positive and negative interactions across baseline and treatment is given below (neutral interactions are not delineated in this data).

Interactions	Baseline	Treatment
Positive	8%	66%
Negative	33%	7%

Note that Barney's mother infrequently engaged in positive interactions with Barney during baseline. An old saying comes to mind, "It's tough to remember to swim in the pool when you keep having to fight off the alligators." She also spent more time in negative interactions with Barney. (*What a surprise!*)

On the other hand, note what happened to parent-child interactions when the intervention is in place. Negative interactions go way down and positive interactions go way up. Again, what a surprise. I thought the experts said that if we use punishment, that we are breaking the bond of love between parent and child. According to them, shouldn't Barney resent his mother's authority?

Could it be that when a parent is effective in managing their child, that all kinds of positive interactions can take place? The use of powerful consequences can make unpleasant situations more pleasant. Ask parents if it is easier to "bond" with their children when they are respectful of designated rules about behavior. It is my contention that the effective use of consequences, punishers included, intensifies the quality of a relationship, not diminishes it.

I want to make one last point about these data. Does it not point to the blunder of examining correlation research data to determine whether parents who use "punitive looking" discipline techniques are the cause or the effect? Did Barney's behavior have something to do with his mother's mood and verbal behavior? When Barney was misbehaving more frequently, what happened? Parental negative interactions go up. When Barney behaved more appropriately, what happened with his mother. She spent way more time being pleasant. Using consequences seemed to have nice side effect for Barney and his mother.

If you surmised that Barney's mother was a mean and vindictive person, as the baseline data might suggest, you might be erroneous. If an effective manner of handling children is present, many mothers and fathers would probably be less "punitive looking?" Even skilled people can be at a loss about how to handle some children, until a systematic plan using consequences is drawn up, as the case below illustrates.

The Case of: "One More Strike and You Are Out!"

Grandmothers raising their children's kids are an ever-increasing family dynamic. At a time in their life when they deserve a rest, some people are raising children they may not be able to keep up with. It is an all too common situation that my behavioral specialists and I have faced. We have worked with some grandmothers who had care taking responsibilities for multiple children from two different daughters. Many times, their daughters, who were often on drugs habitually, get pregnant. While still taking drugs they gave birth to the child, and then either voluntarily or sometimes involuntarily give the child to their mother to raise. Unfortunately they then replicated the process. The worst case we have run across was a grandmother (her husband had passed away) in her 70's raising 12 children, from two daughters. I could not comprehend how anyone, even in great athletic shape, could effectively manage that situation. She needed more than behavior modification for her grandchildren!

We were referred two children from county mental health who were being cared for by their paternal grandmother, Mikki. Mikki had experience with difficult children, having worked in group homes for a while. However, she appeared to be unprepared to effectively deal with her two grandchildren, particularly Antonio, a 10-year-old boy with serious problem behaviors. Antonio's social worker referred him for behavioral services. He had been in counseling before, but no effect was observed on his behavior at home and school.

The county department of mental health was even considering providing an aide for his waking hours, to keep tabs on him. When the referral was made to me, I requested one month to make headway. If my behavioral specialist and I could not bring the level of some of his behaviors down, we agreed to transfer the case to whomever mental health wanted to assign.

The referral information indicated that Antonio had problems with disrespect toward adults, problems at school, and a negative attitude. In fact, he was having extreme difficulty in an after-school program, where he was expelled previously and was admitted back after some persuasion on his behalf by county social workers. Upon our entering the intervention phase, he continued to engage in undesirable behaviors in this after school program. He currently had "five strikes" in this program. A strike represents 3 incidents of disruptive and/or inappropriate behavior in a single day. Unfortunately for us, his next 3 incident day would be his last strike.

But Antonio's behavior in the home also needed our immediate attention. Any parent will tell you that siblings argue. Unfortunately, almost all parents have ascribed this as a fact of nature. But in some families, the rate and intensity of the arguments is substantial (does the phrase– fight like cats and dogs bring to mind a picture). Parents feel that they spend all their time presiding from one argument to the next. If you add in physical aggression as part of the complex, arguing can be a back breaker on some or many days, as it was in the present case.

Simply asking Antonio and his sister to stop arguing, separate them, and intermittently send them to their rooms did not work. The previous strategy to deal with arguments was to figure out who started the argument and why. This strategy often led down the path of no return. Our analysis found that in this case, like many others, it took two to tango.

The plan for addressing this interlocking dynamic was to count each argument against both children, not attempting to find out who started it. An argument required both to say something to each other in a negative or derogatory tone. Then, we taught the grandmother how to use early bedtime as a contingency for unacceptable levels of arguing on a given day. Yes, Virginia, *when* children are to go to bed is a parental prerogative. If it is a parental prerogative, it can be a privilege that is earned. This may be counter to what some experts have told you, but it is a privilege. Also, sending children to bed early as a consequence for their behavior during the day will not cause them to become teenage psychotics. You can see below what it did for Antonio.

During a 1-week baseline period (see first column above), Antonio and his sister argued on the average of three times per day (with a high of five and a low of one argument). The initial period of intervention stipulated an early bedtime consequence for arguments at or above 3. In our contingency, if Antonio and his sister had 2 or fewer arguments in a given day,

Average Frequency of Arguing Across Baseline & Consequence Time Periods						
Baseline	3/8-17	3/18-27	3/28-4/12	4/13-19	4/21-5/4	5/5-14
3.0	1.5	.75	.50	.25	0	0

then they both went to bed at their normal 8 o'clock time period. Note that in the first two-week period (3/8-3/17), the average daily rate of arguing was 1.5. This translates to the two children rarely having three arguments, because you know what kicks in if that happens. The period from 4/21- 5/ 14 did not have one incident of arguing behavior. There are not too many families that can boast that, let alone children who were previously experiencing severe difficulty in dealing with each other without taunting and arguing. It is amazing how much self-control two children, who displayed little control over their emotions previously, can have when you wield a powerful consequence.

With arguing at an extremely reasonable level, we decided to use the same consequence for problems at the after-school program. Instead of waiting for Antonio to reach three incidents, which would have been too late, we set up an early bedtime contingency (for him only) if one incident occurred that day. Remember, he had five strikes, so we could not afford another strike without risking his expulsion from this program. Since inception of this program Antonio did not receive another strike for the remainder of the school year. You can say that Antonio likes to stay up late. What could have been a disaster turned out well in the end. No physically painful consequence was needed, nor was a one-on-one aide for all his waking hours required. Just control bedtime!

• Why do you think a bedtime contingency was so effective in this case?
• Is it a principle of "human nature" that siblings have to fight with each other?

Myth # 5: Time-out Does Not Work

Why is this a Myth?

While the popularity of time-out is widespread, it is often misused by parents to modify child behavior (Cipani, 1999). Everyone claims to have used time-out, and many report it does not work. Why would the results of parents' everyday use of time-out be in stark contrast to the result obtained in numerous research studies? Perhaps the following can be instructive in that regard.

I watched with interest one day when a TV newsmagazine show was covering child problem behavior and a "new" technique to deal with it. Incidentally, I had not seen any research supporting this new technique. The TV program had several parents being interviewed, accompanied with video-clips of their families in chaos. One of the parents claimed that she had tried everything and nothing had worked. The reporter asked her about time-out and she mentioned that her use of that did not work either. The TV program then showed videotape of her and her child as a graphic depiction of what goes on in her house. This boy engaged in a number of problem behaviors such as disobedience and inappropriate social behavior towards his sister. At one point he hits his sister, and as I recall, the mother made some remark like, " Why did you do that?"

Now remember, this is someone who claims that time-out does not work for her children. Is she under the impression that uncovering the reason why a child would hit his sister is a better strategy? If she had not been identified earlier in the video as the parent, I would have assumed she was part of the TV crew, just watching this child go from one incident to the next.

I have a news flash: In order for time-out to "work," you have to use it! Was she waiting for homicide to occur before issuing the proclamation "OK, Bobby, you killed your sister, now you must go to time-out." I have always wished they would have me critique these parenting efforts and then with parental consent, show these people how to use consequences. Time-out is certainly one of the most heavily researched child behavior management techniques. When time-out has been applied correctly as a behavioral contingency, the results have been impressive.

An example of one such pioneering study was conducted in the mid- 1960s (Zeilberger, Sampen, & Sloane, 1968). It was a landmark study for several reasons. First, consider that the standard treatment of child problem behaviors is to have the parent(s) come to a professional's office. The parent and/or child meet with the mental health professional, usually once a week and then go back home until the next appointment. Professionals who work with parents in their home, especially in the 1960s, were about as common as a meteorite landing on a school bus in a major U.S. city.

Rory had been a problem child in his preschool class as well as at home. He engaged frequently in screaming, fighting, disobeying adult instructions and bossing other children around. Rory was 4 years, 8 months old, with an average IQ. The researchers taught Rory's mother how to respond to specific problem behaviors through a designated consequence. The target behaviors selected for a time-out consequence were (1) aggressive behavior in the home and (2) disobedient to parental requests or instructions. The time-out room was one of the family bedrooms that was modified for purposes of deploying a time-out. Toys and other items were taken out of this room. Seven of the 12 steps of the time-out procedure taught to his mother were the following, contingent upon the occurrence of a target behavior:

1. Stating the target misbehavior immediately to Rory. (e.g., "You cannot fight.")
2. Placing him in the time-out room swiftly and without conversation
3. Setting a timer for 2 minutes and requiring him to sit in the time-out area for the entire 2 minutes
4. Leaving him in time-out until tantrum behavior desists for a 2-minute period
5. Ignoring other undesirable behaviors that are not aggressive or disobedient
6. Rewarding Rory when he obeys parental requests
7. Providing special treats for Rory after periods of time when he engages in desirable play

Note that the mother was required to leave Rory in time-out if crying or a tantrum episode occurred prior to the end of the time-out. An episode of tantrum behavior required her to reset the timer for the full 2 minutes. He had to stay in time-out that much longer. Every instance of crying or tantrums in time-out only delayed his release from time-out. Further the mother was also taught to supplement the punishing consequence with reinforcement for appropriate play and following directions.

Time-out was very effective. Prior to the use of time-out, the rate of aggression on some days reached a high of 13 incidents. Following the mother's use of time-out, the rate of aggression dropped considerably. After a rocky first 2 days, all subsequent days using time-out as a consequence had either zero or one occurrence of target behavior per day. Effects to Rory's instruction following behavior also showed the same dramatic change.

These findings are illustrative of what often happens when a parent uses time-out. The first few days can seem worse than before. However, in many cases, once the parent gets over the hurdle of the first few days, time-out is rarely needed. This is the mark of a powerful consequence: it does not need to be implemented that often. The child learns to not engage in the target behavior. Hence the need for implementing the consequence becomes markedly lessened.

This difference in the level of target behavior is usually quite noticeable. What do you think a day feels like when Rory is aggressive 13 times? How different do you think the household is when he is only aggressive once (and goes to time-out)? What about when he is not aggressive at all and follows the majority of his mother's requests? In our clinical use of time-out with many families, we have noted a substantial change in the home atmosphere. Things are much calmer, once problem behavior is reduced to lower levels. It is probably not healthy for parents or children to live in environments that require frequent confrontations between the two. With time-out, my observation suggests that the child often learns what his or her role is and what behaviors are and are not permitted. This makes for a happier home for everyone.

When Should Time-out Be Used?

If one is removing a child from an activity as a contingency for a problem behavior, the removal from that activity must constitute removal from reinforcement. Simply removing a child from an activity, without understanding whether the child finds such an activity inherently pleasing at the time may backfire.

Let us say we have several children who despise math class. The teacher decides that whomever talks during study time will go to time-out. After three days of this contingency, many children are frequenting time-out regularly during math. It is not hard to figure out what has happened. Is time-out during math the consequence that will motivate children not to talk during this period? No, it will have the opposite effect; it will teach children to talk, and subsequently avoid studying. Why? Think about it, which is more preferable to some students, doing nothing or doing math work?

If the context within which one uses time-out were different, the results would be different. Suppose the context is outside recess, and the recess supervisors want to reduce the number of times children throw things outside the school fenced property (on to the street). Do you think a 5- to 8- minute removal from recess will have an effect? What kid does not like recess? Only kids who abhor recess would possibly not be affected by such a contingency. Do you see the distinction? Use of time-out for target behavior during math facts would probably be ineffective. Using time-out for problem behavior during recess would probably be effective. By the way, in order for this to work, recess personnel have to be adept at catching most occurrences. Lack of consistency would lead to lack of results.

What can be done to insure that time-out does not exacerbate the target problem behavior? My suggestion to parents; look and see what is going on when the child is in time-out, and what is going on when the child is returned from the time-out. In my many years of using time-out I have always been encouraged when a child placed in time-out began to cry. Do not misinterpret this. I do not enjoy seeing children cry. Rather, this was a signal to me that the child was leaving a preferred activity and being moved to a less preferred event, time-out.

Are There Any Children Who Love Time-out?

Children can love time-out if it constitutes removal from an unpleasant environment. Determining if removal from an activity constitutes removal of reinforcement is necessary for time-out to be effective. The removal from a non-reinforcing environment has disastrous results on child behavior (Solnick, Rincover, & Peterson, 1977). In this study, the researchers began by using a time-out contingency for tantrums in a six-year-old girl with autism. However, what resulted was probably unexpected. Time-out was not just ineffective at reducing tantrums, but tantrums actually increased. Time-out was not a punishing consequence in this case. Rather, time-out served as a reinforcer for tantrums, increasing their rate.

How could this be? As you may now know, time-out does not always function as a punishing consequence. Solnick and colleagues took this opportunity to uncover some basic principles in how time-out works. They noted that the girl would go to time-out and then engage in self-stimulatory or ritualistic behavior, repeatedly weaving her fingers in a pattern. During instruction, this type of ritualistic behavior was obviously discouraged. So it became an easy choice for her of where to be if one wanted to engage in such behaviors: time-out. She learned that a tantrum resulted in her removal from the instructional task, which was probably not high on her list of things to do. Further to add icing to the cake, she is placed in the time-out area, where she could entertain herself to her hearts content. Could this have been the factor responsible for time-out not working in her situation?

Scientists prefer evidence to speculation. To test this hypothesis, the researchers implemented two more time-out experimental conditions with this girl. Suppose she is sent to time-out but then physically prohibited from engaging in self-stimulatory behavior. Would time-out regain its ability to punish behavior like so many other studies have shown? To test this, in one experimental condition such ritualistic behaviors were restrained immediately. In the other experimental condition the child was not restrained from engaging in the ritualistic behavior during time-out.

As you can imagine, if going to time-out meant free access to hand weaving, then this girl was apparently all in favor of going to lots of time-outs. However, if going to time-out meant that she could not engage in such behavior while there, time out lost its appeal to her. When ritualistic behavior in time-out was restrained, the rate of tantrums was reduced to zero on four of the six sessions. When time-out did not involve restraining her from engaging in ritualistic behavior, tantrums were far more frequent. When time-out spelled free access to hand weaving, she had 16 trips one day to the "land of pleasure".

In short, time-out may not be effective if the child can engage in a preferred activity that she or he can only do when in time-out. Additionally, time-out is also ineffective if it provides an escape from an unpleasant activity (such as chores or homework assignments). If you are given a task that you absolutely hate, behaviors that produce temporary removal of the task become more probable. For example, if your boss delineates a contingency between some behavior and having to leave the office and go to the break room for at least 25 minutes, then your boss has just set a premium on engaging in that behavior.

Time-out may be boring but it beats doing work. Can you see how this might apply to many children in a school setting? In a second phase of their experiment (Solnick et al., 1977), time-out was used with a student for spitting and self abuse during an instructional activity. When such behaviors resulted in this student being removed from the task to time-out, heightened rates of these behaviors (mean of 92 occurrences) resulted. However, time-out was very effective in reducing these behaviors when it resulted in his removal from a play period with lots of toys. The same time-out procedure in this latter condition resulted in the rates of these behaviors decreasing to *zero* within the first few sessions. Now that is what I call an effective consequence!

My question to you: Is time-out a punisher? Your answer: It depends. When it is used as a consequence for misbehaviors during a non-preferred task or activity, your answer is "No, it is not a punisher." When it is used as a consequence for misbehaviors during a play period, your is answer is, "Yes, it functions as a punisher with most kids." This principle holds true for many children across many families and school environments.

The Case of: "I Hope You Learned Your Lesson!"

I was a consultant to a family whose 4-year-old son had Down's Syndrome. He was in a preschool class, but was having difficulty in this program. The family wanted to know whether anything could be done to improve his behavior at school. I went to observe him at his preschool in Sacramento one bright sunny morning, with consent from school personnel. While the school staff seemed to like him, they were not sure that he could remain in this mainstream program because of his "behavioral difficulties."

When I arrived, he and his classmates were listening to the teacher give a lesson on prepositions. They had a big plastic tube (the ones that children can walk through) in the middle of the classroom. A child was called up to get in a position relative to this tube. For example, one child was told to get "behind the tube." The other children were supposed to be watching and learning. My client of course was more interested in the girl sitting next to him and her ponytails. After being repeatedly told to watch and learn, in order to "distract" him from playing with her hair, he was called upon to now stand in front of, behind and, to the side, of the tube. It was apparent to everyone (probably him as well) that he did not know behind, inside and other prepositions. He just waited for the teaching staff to move him to where he was supposed to go.

Following this exercise, he sat down, and picked up where he left off: playing with this girl's hair. Apparently the 20th time of bothering this girl was the contingency for time-out. The teacher's aide directed him to time-out. She explained to him why he was placed in time-out and then was told to sit there until he could come out and participate in the learning situation. Guess where the time-out was? Next to the toy shelf. Guess where the aide went? Back to the circle. Guess what my client did while he was in "time-out?" He began playing with the toys. He must have mistaken the directive. He must have thought they said, "play in time-out!" instead of, "stay in time-out." I would venture to guess that the school staff would probably have told me that time-out does not work for him. Small wonder!

- What lesson was the child learning from the time-out plan?
- Did it affect his motivation to attend to the lesson?

What Are Some of the Parameters of an Effective Use of Time-out?

As mentioned above, time-out has to involve the removal of a reinforcing event or activity. Time-outs during tasks or chores the child dislikes will not function as a punishing consequence. Further, effective use of time-out requires adherence to the basic principles of punishment, to be delineated in Section III. There are several additional parameters one needs to consider in using time-out: (1) location of time-out area, (2) duration of time-out, (3) criteria for release, (4) preventing early unauthorized escape from time-out, and (5) providing reinforcement upon returning from time-out.

Location of time-out area. Location, location, location. It is not just a catchy phrase for real estate ads. The importance of the time-out location, if it involves removal from an activity and area, makes all the difference in the world. After all, one would not use a candy store as a time-out area. "OK, Franco, you did not come inside when I called you. Therefore, you must spend 15 minutes in this candy store for not complying with my request in a timely manner." You can hear Franco plead, "Oh please dad, I think I will need 25 minutes in time-out to really learn my lesson."

When I teach parents how to use time-out, we first agree on which behavior, or possibly two behaviors, will produce time-out. We also agree to make the time-out inevitable when the target behavior occurs. Additionally, the advent of time-out must be relatively soon after the behavior has occurred. If a parent usually has to argue with his or her child, the parent will be taught to physically guide the child to time-out. (*Note to reader- this is where a competent behavior analyst may have to make a judgment about whether time-out can be deployed in a given case.*) If the parent seems unwilling or unable to get the child to time-out maybe due to size or fear of a retaliatory response, another consequence might be preferable.

Once all those formalities have been settled, the parent will take the child to an area void of entertaining stimuli and traffic. Areas for time-out that are nixed by me include the TV room, near the playroom, in the kitchen (high traffic area), and usually the bedroom. If the bedroom is to be used, the door is to be left open and the parent must be willing to supervise the child while she or he sits on the bed.

Yes, that is right! The parent must be willing to sit and watch and make sure the child does not engage in any pleasurable activity. When you hear parents say time-out does not work, ask them where the child is sent. If they say to his bedroom, ask them if they close the door when the child is in time-out. If the answer is "yes," you can guess why time-out does not work with this child!

Length of time-out. The length of time-out is another consideration. Many personnel who teach parents to use time-out have the 1-minute for every year rule. A child of age 3 would therefore have time-outs that last for 3 minutes, a child of age 6 would receive 6 minutes of time-out and an elderly gentleman of 77 in a nursing facility would have to endure 77 minutes! This "rule" is one that people made up, with no basis in fact. In research studies, time-outs as short as 10 seconds have been effective at reducing target behavior. However, other research studies have shown the efficacy of time-outs that lasted 3 hours. Will 10-second time-out plans always work? Probably not. Time-out duration should be of sufficient length to be effective, yet not be unnecessarily long.

I have developed several considerations when designating the length of the time-out period. I base the length of time on two factors: (1) the release criteria from time-out, which I will detail shortly, and (2) how often the behavior occurs. If I am dealing with a target behavior that occurs several times per hour, I want the time-out to be relatively shorter. Why? So that the child may leave time-out and be faced with the opportunity to either engage in appropriate behavior, which does not produce time-out, or engage in the target behavior, and be sent to time-out again. The greater the number of opportunities to learn this the better. For such instances, time-outs of several minutes are sufficient. With behaviors that occur infrequently, the length of time-out can be longer.

Release criteria. The manner in which the time-out is ended can take one of two forms: time contingent release or response contingent release. In the former, the elapse of the designated amount of time determines when the child is returned to the activity from time-out. For example, if the time-out length was 5 minutes, once that has elapsed, the child is returned. However, one caveat to this time contingency needs to also be stipulated.

Five minutes to me means 5 consecutive, continuous minutes in the time-out area, whether it be a seat or carpet square area. If a child gets up, as was the case with our client in the preschool class, he should be returned to time-out. Further, the time-out period should begin over again! How many times have you seen the following: Child is put in time-out. She gets up and wanders over to the play area. The adult says, "Now Betina have you learned your lesson?" Yes, she has! Whenever she gets tired of time-out, she can simply get up and end that event. What is wrong with that? Time-out is not supposed to be a phenomenon that is terminated once the child is bored with it. Loss of fun activities, for a designated period of time, is how time-out produces its effect.

It turns out that this is not just my opinion and experience with time-out. A research study with 24 children, ages 2 to 6, examined the efficacy of two different types of time-outs (Bean & Roberts, 1981). In one form of time-out, the parent determines when the child is released from time-out. In the second form of time-out, the child determines when she or he is ready to end time-out.

One group of parents used time-out for noncompliance, with the release being contingent on remaining in time-out for 2 continuous minutes and quiet for the last 15 seconds. This group was called the parent release group. The second group, called the child release group, was also sent to time-out for noncompliance. However, according to the Dreikur's model (see Dreikur & Grey, 1968), when the child felt ready to "do as you are told," the child could leave time-out. The basic comparison in this study was over who chooses when time-out is ended. Should it be the parent aided with an understanding of how to provide effective consequences, or the child, aided in the pursuit of the pleasure principle? The results should not surprise you. The parent release group improved from an average level of compliance to parent commands of 23.4% in baseline to 77.9% following the time-out usage by parents.

The child release group improved from 23.3% to 44.1%, not as large an improvement. In fact, consider looking at these results in the following framework. When a child determines when she or he gets out of time-out, the child is only compliant with one of every two commands given (i.e., about 44% of the time). Contrast that with three of four commands being followed for the parent release group.

The response contingent release form of time-out requires that the child not engage in some behavior, such as tantrums, for some period of time prior to release. In the study above, the child was required to be quiet for the last 15 seconds of the 2-minute time-out period before being released. If the child screamed right before the 2 minutes were up, the time-out period was extended until the 15-second criterion was met.

As you can imagine, especially in the beginning of implementing a response contingent release time-out, time-outs will often last longer than the initial requirement. In some cases, a 2-minute time-out can last 25 minutes the first time. However, for the overwhelming majority of clients from my clinical practice with whom I have used this form of time-out, within 1-2 days of using time-out, the length approximates the initial value. The children learn it is not in their best interest to tantrum or scream while in time-out, for it only prolongs it. The children learn to accept the consequence and move on once it is done.

What is the purpose behind the response contingent release? I have no data to support my argument that a response contingent release is more effective than a simple time-elapse release. But I prefer the response contingent release form of time-out, because it also teaches compliance while in time-out. If time-out truly has removed a reinforcing activity, then the longer the removal from the activity is incurred, the more motivated the child is to leave time-out. When parents remark that their child might stay in time-out a long time screaming, I tell them the following. Time is on your side (see, even the Rolling Stones understood this maxim). Eventually the child will stop and learn that screaming gets him or her nowhere.

But why does it take some children longer to figure this out? If a child wants to leave time-out, why would he or she engage in screaming and tantrum behavior? It is not in the child's best interest to do so. Children scream because this is the way they usually terminate activities and things they do not want. If someone turns off their TV program, they tantrum and scream. If they are told they cannot have ice cream, they scream until their parent "gives in." When they are in situations not to their liking, their supercomputer brain is busy at work. Their databases are firing away, coming up with plausible scenarios of how to deal with their dilemma. After all this electro-chemical activity, the result pops up. Yep, after this extensive search of all similar circumstances and outcomes, screaming is your best bet here. Do that, it is likely to work. Scream, and scream loud, especially if other behavioral efforts have failed to impress mom or dad.

I do not want to add screaming as an adaptive way to get out of time-out. And unfortunately, if they scream the entire time they are in time-out, what do you think they learn? Scream for 2 minutes and you get released. They may be unaware that you planned to release them regardless of what they were doing. They may superstitiously learn that screaming terminates time-out, like it does so many other unpleasant events.

The response contingent form of release from time-out teaches children that screaming is not an adaptive response to this situation. Even though I know this is difficult for some parents to stick to, I feel we need to draw a line in the sand. This can often be your first test to stick to consequences for tantrum behavior. Consider it a test you must pass.

Preventing unauthorized escape from time-out. When a child attempts to get out of time-out before the release criteria has been met, the efficacy of time-out is compromised as demonstrated in previous research. Does the way a parent deals with attempted escapes from time-out affect the capability of that consequence to act as a punisher? You bet! A study compared several parental reactions to escape attempts from time-out on the frequency of escape attempts (Roberts & Powers, 1990). In other words, does the way a parent react to the child leaving time-out affect such escape behaviors during time-out?

One group of parents was taught to spank their child when their child attempted to get out of the chair time-out (called spank group). In another group, the parents were taught to hold (restrain) their child in the chair (called hold group). In a third group, parents were taught to place their child in an empty room, with a 4 foot high plywood board blocking the exit, physically preventing them from leaving (called barrier group). These three groups required the child to remain a certain amount of time in time-out and also the child's release from time-out was response contingent.

Which of the three groups had the least number of escape attempts from time-out? The percentage of children exhibiting excessive escape attempts in each group was the following: Spank group 33%, hold group 56%, and barrier group 17%. The barrier condition resulted in the fewest number of children attempting to continually get out of time-out. In contrast, the hold group was an ineffective and exhausting procedure for dealing with escape attempts. Preventing escape is a logistical concern for the implementation of time-out by parents. Again, some parents may need the aide of a competent behavior analyst to help them with this aspect.

Reinforcement following return from time-out. I also teach parents that when the child returns from time-out, catch her or him being good. It is important to have this contrast: hit sister, go to time-out. Play nicely, get a hug from mom. Do not continue to ignore appropriate behavior once the child is back from time-out. If there is this contrast between what you do when your child is in time-out and what you do when your child is not, you will get a nice effect from time-out.

I remember working at one of the Head Start classes where we were using time-out on children who would aggress against their peers. One of the 4-year-old boys, who was escorted by me to time-out, was not a happy Head Start camper. He sat defiantly in time-out, and upon completing his time requirement, returned to the same activity that started his trouble before. I can remember him looking at me as if, well you can guess. His glistening stare told the whole story. He was not used to being punished for such behavior (and unfortunately was a frequent aggressor). As a side note, I believe the purpose of that stare was: "Don't mess with me again."

I was working with the teacher responsible for this boy and the other children in his group. I think most people would have been hesitant to become involved with him again, and would have stayed clear of him. I knew he was going to present a problem to the teachers, in terms of enacting time-out. If he made me apprehensive, I could only imagine what the teachers felt when he stared them down. Luckily a voice beckoned to me: "Catch him being good." I watched him play with the other children and then a perfect opportunity was laid in front of me. He had just shared with one of the other children a toy matchbox car. I scurried over to him and said, "Wow, both of you are really playing nice together. I like the way you are sharing these cars (looking straight at him)." You could see the ice melt and a beaming smile took its place. For the remainder of my observation in that class, I cannot recount him aggressing further. I never forgot the lesson that 4-year-old taught me about the importance of what adults do when a child returns from time-out. By the way, his mother stopped me a few days subsequent to his visit to time-out (by me) and thanked me. She said, "You know he needs to be straightened out. He can be too controlling and mean." I thought, "Yes ma'am, I know where you are coming from. I saw it in his eyes."

An effective punisher very often makes other behaviors more probable. Do not miss this opportunity to reinforce acceptable behaviors subsequent to the child being placed in time-out no matter how odd it may feel.

What Are the Implications of a Response-contingent Release of Time-out?

I also believe there is another benefit of this form of time-out. In the overwhelming majority of cases, the child learns to eventually accept time-out without much resistance. If a child learns to accept time-out without generating additional outbursts, it will be easier for others to use time-out, or some other similar punisher, with your child. Why is this important? Children who get into serious trouble at school often get to that level not as a result of the initial incident. It was the child's response to a levied consequence that resulted in the parent being called to the principal's office to come pick up their child.

Harry, a fictitious student, receives a math assignment from his ninth grade teacher. He is in a funny mood, so he tries to pick the paper up with his mouth. The other kids are laughing hysterically. Harry's teacher tells him that his display of lunacy cost him five minutes of recess time. At the mention of loss of recess time, Harry calls her a word that rhymes with witch. (*Note to reader: his cerebral data bank told him that will improve his chances to get the five minutes restored.*) Oops, Houston we have a problem. Maybe such a response works at home with mom, but not in school! Of course that response winds him in the principal's office, with a threat of a sexual harassment charge possibly being filed. His mother is called for this serious behavioral incident.

His mother is not meeting with the principal of the school because Harry acted silly. If he had accepted his consequences, that would have ended it. She is pleading for her child's educational life, under threat of expulsion, because of his response to the consequence. More often than not, it is best to accept those initial consequences rather than engage in more debilitating behaviors. The development of this understanding in children, I believe, requires additional effort on our part. An additional contingency is often needed when these debilitating behaviors occur during the time-out period, hence my strong preference for response contingent releases.

I believe parents need to teach their children early in life that consequences are inevitable when certain behaviors occur. By teach, I do not mean preach one thing and practice the opposite. The child will learn this by your following through on consequences to behavior. The child will learn that escalation of her or his behavior will not minimize the consequence in the least. Children need a parent who does more than provide a lecture to them about accepting consequences. They need someone who enforces the policy. That is how they really learn this lesson.

Why Does Time-out Not Work for Many Parents?

If you are getting the message that many people who claim time-out does not work are the same people who misuse it, you are an astute reader of my sarcasm. To reiterate, time-out has worked great in research studies where all these concerns have been addressed. It has not worked as great when people who are not apprised of these parameters have deployed it for their child's misbehavior. If a person's definition of time-out is moving a child to a corner, you should tell them to read and re-read this section many times. Time-out can be successful, but it takes some basic understanding of the reasons behind its effectiveness and issues related to its implementation. To learn more about how to use time-out effectively, please consult the relevant chapter in my book, *Helping Parents Help Their Kids: A Clinical Guide to Six Child Problem Behavior* (Cipani, 1999).

What Can Be Used for Older Children, in Place of Time-out?

With teenagers, their access to privileges can supplant time-out. For the occurrence of a specific target behavior, privileges are lost that day or evening. If the target behavior does not occur, or occurs relatively infrequently, the child or adolescent earns privileges. Further, this type of consequence can be used in a manner that gradually teaches the child self-control with respect to a given behavior. This is accomplished by tying a certain criterion level of behavior to accessing privileges. Going above the criterion for that day results in loss of evening privileges; staying at or below that level results in privileges available that day/evening.

Let us say we have an adolescent that does not comply with his parent's simple directives. His mother may ask him to throw his empty soda cans in the trash, or pick his socks up off the floor, and other similar demands. His rate of compliance is low, as reported by his mother. She claims he rarely follows through with her requests. Only if she threatens him with telling his father of his insolence when his father gets home does he sometimes shape up. (Yes the old, "wait till your father gets home," ploy.) But even that is not full proof. Given that his compliance is low, it also means that his noncompliance is high. Let us say we measure the rate of noncompliance each day for a 1-week period. The following data is collected.

Day	Number of non-compliant incidents
Monday	7
Tuesday	6
Wednesday	8
Thursday	11
Friday	10

If you review these results, you see that this child is noncompliant to parental requests. He had a low of 6 non-compliant incidents on Wednesday and a high of 11 on Thursday. We select the criterion that no more than 7 occurrences of noncompliance in a given day earns him access to privileges. On days when he exceeds this level of noncompliance, he will lose out on privileges. The data on noncompliance for the next week reveals that he clearly knows where the line is.

Day	Number of non-compliant incidents
Monday	5
Tuesday	4
Wednesday	6
Thursday	5
Friday	6

As he achieved access to the privilege readily for 5 straight days, the criterion is moved down a few incidents to five or less. The result for the third week is given below.

Day	Number of non-compliant incidents
Monday	3
Tuesday	4
Wednesday	6 (lost privileges that evening)
Thursday	2
Friday	4

He reaches the criterion for success on 4 of the 5 days. But it is important to note what the effect of the loss of privileges on Wednesday was on the next day's performance. He had his best day. I'll bet he said to himself the morning after the loss of privileges, "Boy I do not want to lose TV and going out with my friends again tonight." Loss of privileges effects behavior change in this adolescent.

I have used loss of privileges for many of the cases that we have worked on across a 2-decade period. Sometimes it is loss of TV time, sometimes it is loss of video rentals on the weekends, or playing with friends after homework is done, and in a few cases, loss of the family car for the weekend (obviously these were kids of driving age).

Sometimes, what you use as a contingent event takes a lot of ingenuity and thought. It requires that you always watch what activities or items interest your child. When you see children doing some activity everyday, of their own accord, think contingent privilege. Let me give you a case in point. One day I was paid to do an in-service for a local elementary school in Stockton in the early 1980s. Several teachers were having problems managing some of their students, and the principal had been referred to me as "the behavior modifier."

I arrived early for my workshop after the school day was over. The principal was tied up with someone on the phone so I was told to wait in the office. The bell rang, signaling the end of the school day. To my surprise, a hoard of kids headed for the principal's office, of their own choice. They went right to a pencil machine in the corner and began inserting nickels into the machine. Some kids must have been burning the midnight oil studying because they apparently needed six, seven or even eight pencils. The line eventually disappeared, but not before the pencil machine had seen a whirlwind of activity. "Strange," I thought to myself.

I was invited into the office, and after some pleasantries I asked in a puzzled manner, "What is it with the kids buying pencils?" The principal proudly boasted, "That pencil machine is really going to help the PTA. You see every fourth or fifth pencil dispensed, on average, has a Pac-Man insignia on the pencil. The kids just keep putting nickels in." My first thought was "The next time I get invited to this school, the school staff are probably going to want me to give a talk entitled, "The treatment of kids with a pencil-buying addiction: The next crisis in children's mental health." All kidding aside, my immediate thought was the following. The power this machine had could certainly be used more effectively. How? A contingent relationship could be established after collecting some baseline data. For example, anyone with a behavioral incident would lose 2 to 4 consecutive days of buying privileges in the office or school store. The more adroit a parent or teacher becomes at spotting unique but powerful consequences, and learns to use them, the more the child will exert self-control over problem behaviors. Watch the kids, their behavior will lead the way.

Section III:
Six Basic Principles of Punishment

It should be evident that outcome-oriented punishment adheres to some basic principles that distinguish it from consequences that are ineffective. The following principles of effective punishment are drawn from a list of 14 principles that were enumerated by two psychologists, Drs. Azrin and Holz (1966). Their presentation of these 14 principles was based on numerous research studies in animal laboratories and some experimental research with humans at the time. Since that time, research studies testing the efficacy of various behavioral contingencies have supported these principles.

I have selected five principles of effective punishment, from their list. I have also added one: Prove it works with children. These six principles are most relevant for consideration when using procedures that may function as punishment to change child behavior.

- Principle I: There Must Exist a Behavioral Contingency
- Principle II: Be Consistent
- Principle III: The "Even Swap" Rule
- Principle IV: Remove Competing Consequences
- Principle V: Be Specific
- Principle VI: Prove It Works

Principle I: There Must Exist a Behavioral Contingency

What is a behavioral contingency? At the heart of outcome-oriented punishment is the behavioral contingency. Put simply, a behavioral contingency is a reliable temporal relationship between a specific behavior and a consequence. You may have heard this referred to as an, "If ___, then ___," statement. For example, if you eat your peas, then you can have dessert. Conversely, if you don't eat your peas, then you don't get your dessert. Similarly, if you brush your teeth, then you can go outside. Conversely, if you do not brush your teeth, then you cannot go outside. Both of these are examples of behavioral contingencies, a temporal relationship between a behavior and some event that follows it reliably (i.e., a consequence).

In order for a punishment effect to occur, a reliable link between the specific behavior and the intended consequence has to exist. Further, this reliable relationship produces a lowered level of the behavior (i.e., punishment). If a parent removes the child's dessert whenever she fails to eat her peas in a given period of time, its effect on behavior determines whether punishment has occurred. Let me use a hypothetical example to illustrate a behavioral contingency involving punishment.

What Happens On the Planet Freudania?

Let's say we have an alien family who has just beamed down from the fictitious planet Freudania. They have taken custody of an Earth child they found in the woods. (*Note to reader: I need you to go with me on this.*) In attempting to uncover child-rearing approaches on earth, they initially formulate the policy of letting the child guide their practice. They say to each other, "Let's see what she does and then we can determine how Earth parents raise their children." They set this practice in motion, allowing her to engage in whatever behavior she desires. For example, at mealtime, they allow this child to eat food in whatever order she desires. To their amazement she eats the dessert first and always leaves the vegetables. Of course, they have heard this is not wise, nutritionally. They are surprised to see the lack of self-responsibility on the part of this child. This is quite in contrast to Freudania children, who after going through the Oedipal-Erectus stage of development, are quite responsible and need no direction from parents in their daily life. In fact, on Freudania, parents can only get in the way of their child's development, by interfering with their natural growth toward good. It is therefore best to let the child be himself or herself.

Alas such is not the case with these Earth children. After 7 weeks of this failed policy, they conclude that they must try something else. After becoming attentive listeners to a variety of afternoon talk shows, they surmise that earth children are responsive to logic and reasoning. If they are told why something is good for them, they will "see the light," and will start eating their vegetables. They remark to each other, "Boy that sure is easy. Why did we not see that in the beginning. Before each mealtime, we will reason with this Earth child, providing her with a nice discussion on the long-term value of eating vegetables." They proceed in earnest. During their discussions with this child, they go all out to show her the benefits of eating vegetables. They cite data, show her charts, and describe what she will look like if she eats vegetables. They even provide her with testimony from actresses who ate their vegetables when they were her age and now have million-dollar modeling and acting contracts. After another 7 weeks, to their surprise, this does not generate much in the way of their adopted daughter eating vegetables. However, it does seem to encourage a lot of arguing, excuses, and crying fits from her. Maybe they failed to comprehend what the people on the talk shows said this strategy was good for. Perhaps this is how Earth trains their young early in life for a legal career! One day they pick up a book, which seems to promote an alternate method to get their daughter to finally start eating her vegetables. This book teaches them to designate the relationship between getting dessert and eating vegetables to be one of a contingency. First vegetables, then dessert. As a

> result of this practice over the next 7 weeks the vegetables are no longer left on the plate. They are elated at their daughter's progress. Apparently on Earth, one must get the behavior to occur, before giving out the preferred event. Again, such is not a behavioral principle on Freudania.

Unlike Freudania, on the third rock from the sun, the principle of a behavioral contingency forms the basis for scientific demonstrations of the efficacy of consequences. The behavioral contingency is to the understanding of human behavior as DNA is to the field of genetics. Many studies in the last 7 decades have used the behavioral contingency as the basis for studying what causes behavior to change. The strength of this field, called behavior analysis, was, and is, its reliance on an accumulation of scientific evidence prior to building hypotheses and theories about effective treatments. It is important to note that a theory of punishment developed out of research data demonstrating the effectiveness of certain behavioral contingencies to reduce the rate of behavior. This runs contrary to the usual manner in which traditional psychological theories proceed. In most other theories of human behavior, scholars come up with elaborate hypotheses and theories that attempt to explain real life behavioral phenomenon before an empirical basis is established.

I remember as an undergraduate in the early 1970s, that some psychology professors were less than impressed with the applications of behavioral principles of reinforcement and punishment to human behavior. A comment from a fictitious Professor Freud-Jung may have been along the following line: "That behavior mod stuff only works for animals. You would not want to use it for real life problems with children."

When I inquired why this behavior mod stuff could not work with human subjects, I would got a frown, followed by a scowl. In the professor's line of reasoning, changing human behavior should be made more complex. How simple minded of me to even raise such a question! Dr. Freud-Jung might have responded to my question in the following manner, "This type of model is too simple. You mean all one has to do to help parents help their kids is to determine what procedures increase behavior and what procedures decrease behavior? That is not realistic. Something really deep is at the root of child problems." Yes, I noted, something was getting really deep!

As the saying goes, simple is better. The simplicity of this focus (i.e., how to increase and decrease behavior) is all one often needs to help parents. For example, Mrs. Riccardo (fictitious character) tells the school psychologist that her son does not study like he should. What is the presenting problem in its basic form? What is this mother wanting help with? Her child does not study enough, and she would like him to study more. This is a problem requiring the use of factors that increase that behavior. Anything that does not contribute to that analysis is extra baggage, no matter how impressed the proponent of the "deep analysis" believes his or her colleagues would be.

What Happens When People Use Consequences Haphazardly?

I once heard someone say, "Yeah, I use that behavior mod stuff. When my kid misbehaves, I give him a time-out." While this may sound like a behavioral contingency, it is a deceptive impostor. What constitutes misbehavior? If a specific behavior is not delineated, then the parent's judgment about the child's misbehavior is required. Do you think that there will be consistency over a 2- week period in applying time-out to a uniform behavior? Not likely. Early researchers did not reinforce the rat when it looked like it was engaged in purposeful actions. That might have constituted everything from bar pressing to voiding in the cage. As you can imagine, the rat would never have "figured out" what single behavior produced food and might have been forced to engage in some pretty wacky routines. Similarly, a behavioral contingency plan that requires an adult to detect accurately when the child is misbehaving is not something you want to bet on.

This lack of stipulating a behavioral contingency is what I term a haphazard use of consequences. It is quite often the case in everyday efforts to change child behavior. Many parents, when resorting to *behavior mod*, attempt to modify many undesirable behaviors of their child all in one shot. I call this the, "let's fix everything, because I only want to do this once," approach to raising kids. Subsequently, instead of focusing on one target behavior, the parent wants to use a designated consequence for everything under the rubric of, "If it pisses me off, it is misbehavior, and I will send him to his room."

Let's take the hypothetical case of Mr. and Mrs. Ringer. They have decided to use time-out to deal with their almost 4-year-old, defiant daughter, Vanessa. They report they will put her in the corner when she needs it. Obviously they did not think through what specific behavior will be targeted. They believe that they will be best served by going with their gut instinct at the time. Whenever they think Vanessa has behaved badly, she will get a time-out.

What does a gut instinct approach to consequences look like? The first time Mr. Ringer gave his daughter a time-out, it was immediately following a verbal defiance of his request to pick up her toys. The next time Vanessa was sent to time-out when she threw a toy in the house. Her father remarked, "She should have known better, and did this to spite me, so I'll teach her!" Subsequently, two noncompliant acts occurred, to two requests to get a broom, and such did not generate a time-out. When questioned about the apparent discrepancy, Mr. Ringer considered these noncompliant acts mild in comparison to the verbal defiance she displayed earlier. Later that day, Vanessa refused to go take her nap. She argued back and forth with Mrs. Ringer until Vanessa shouted, "no, you poopy." This was followed by a time-out.

How consistent are the Ringers? My answer is, "How can one be consistent with something so encompassing as any misbehavior?" As you can see, making a decision about whether a set of behaviors constitutes something as broad as misbehavior is fraught with problems. Deploying time-out for a child's misbehavior may sound good in theory, but it stinks in practice.

What should the Ringers have done? The Ringers might have sat down and determined which misbehavior they wanted to concentrate on first. Let us say that they both decide to use time-out only when Vanessa calls them names of a derogatory nature (e.g., "poopy," "you're stupid," "you brat," and of course the double whammy, "You are a stupid poopy."). Other behaviors will not result in time-out (yet). Only derogatory names. Each time she says something that is in that class of behaviors, she will be placed in time-out. Now a specific behavior produces a specific consequence (i.e., a behavioral contingency exists). If Vanessa makes a derogatory comment, she will go to time-out for 4 minutes. The research study described below illustrates the principle of specifying a behavioral contingency.

Subjective vs. Objective Targets Makes All the Difference in the World!

Can adults use subjective judgments about a phenomenon as the basis for delivering a punishing consequence? I cannot say always, but it is a sure bet that more often than not, one will not achieve the desired level of behavior change. A study that made a comparison between consequences for specific target behaviors versus consequences based on subjective judgment sheds scientific evidence on this issue (White & Bailey, 1990).

Let's say you are a physical education (PE) teacher in an elementary school and are faced regularly with children in two of your gym classes who engage in the following three classes of disruptive behaviors. First, they do not comply with your requests to engage in some activity or exercise. Second, the students hit other children while you are trying to explain some sport or exercise to them. Third, they throw stuff at each other when you are not looking. We have all been in PE classes as children and probably remember some classes that were in a state of havoc daily. The PE teacher's job in managing children is complicated by the inherent fact that PE class often takes place in an outside environment.

Such was the case in a Tallahassee elementary school in the late 1980s. Behavioral researchers Alicia White and Dr. Jon Bailey consulted with a PE teacher who designated two classes that he needed help with. They decided to conduct a study, pitting the effectiveness of a behavioral contingency against an approach that provides consequences based on an overall appraisal of the student's behavior. The latter approach can be likened to the "I will go with my gut instinct," approach.

In the worst of the two classes, the rates of these reported problem behaviors were collected in a baseline condition (i.e., conditions that were typically in effect). These researchers merely counted the occurrence of the three classes of problem behaviors, but did not provide any additional help or advice. The rate of occurrence of these behaviors in 10-minute observations taken over a several day period was between 130 and 343 (a mean of 219 occurrences). No wonder the teacher was asking for help. Most people would be begging to quit!

Following the collection of this data the teacher decided to try something on his own. He attempted to change the children's behavior by using a rating system for each child during the class period. Each child was rated by the teacher as super, good, fair, or poor, in regards to four categories: respecting adults and peers, listening to and following directions, keeping hands and/or feet to self, and reporting incidents to teacher. In other words, the teacher was to judge each child as to his or her level of misbehavior for that gym period, and give each child a super, good, fair or poor rating. The primary consequence of a child obtaining a poor rating was loss of a free play period later in the week and/or a parent conference or visit to the principal.

To the untrained eye this may look like a behavioral contingency. If you are bad (i.e., rating of poor) for the gym period, you will lose your free play (supposed punishing consequence). Right? Wrong. There is no specific behavior that produces the loss of free play. Rather, it is comprised of an ever-changing constellation of behaviors.

What was the effect of this intervention on the rate of the disruptive behaviors? In the worst class, the mean rate of disruptive behaviors for the ten-minute period of observation was now down to 98.5. While this is better than before, this still represents a class that has significant problems. It is obvious there is still plenty of room for improvement. Could a behavioral contingency improve on that? It is time to put up or keep quiet, right?

The behavioral contingency developed by the researchers to address the still high rates of disruptive behaviors in the two classes was called "sit and watch". The following behaviors were to produce the sit and watch consequence: (1) failure to comply with teacher request by initiating movement within 5 seconds of instruction, (2) hitting others, and (3) throwing things at others. Contingent on the occurrence of any of the above behaviors the child was instructed to take a timer and go to an area away from the activity and sit and watch for 3 minutes. Additional consequences were added to the sit and watch procedure for the first class as an additional means of decreasing such behaviors. If the child went to sit and watch once during the period, she or he would lose daily computer time. If the child went to sit and watch more than once during the same period she or he also lost a free play period once every two weeks. If the child engaged in disruptive behavior during sit and watch, she or he lost free play that day. Finally if someone talked to a child in sit and watch, that child also got to experience it.

How did this specific behavioral contingency affect the rate of disruptive behavior relative to the rating system? The mean rate of disruptive behaviors for the first class was 4.6 over the period of the study. What a difference a behavioral contingency can make! Now one has a class that is manageable. The difference between a behavior producing a consequence versus using a judgment about the child's behavior as the basis for consequences can make all the difference in the world.

Principle II: Be Consistent

Who would deny that parents should be consistent in disciplining their child? Everyone believes in consistency. This is a principle that people verbally profess upon cue, but such verbal commitment does not often translate into practice. I believe many people who say they are consistent really believe they are. However, they think of consistency as a phenomenon above 50%. Here's what I mean by consistency.

When I was an undergraduate majoring in psychology, one of my professors said the following in a lecture stressing consistency. "When the subject performs the target behavior, the consequence must be inevitable. If this, then this implies the concept of inevitability." The concept of inevitability certainly does not say, if this then maybe this. The early animal research this professor cited, demonstrating the effectiveness of punishment certainly produced inevitable consequences for a target behavior (Azrin, 1960; Azrin, Holz, & Hake, 1963).

When I am called in to consult on a case where a behavioral plan has already been tried and has failed, I remember those words. I ask myself, "From everything you have seen is the contingency inevitable?" Many times the answer is, "the contingency is unreliable, at best."

This is an example of an inevitable contingency: If you hit your sister, you will go to time-out. Contrast that statement with the following example: If you hit your sister you might go to time-out, unless you apologize, begin crying, or claim you have a stomach pain. Also, if it is Thursday, that is the time-out holiday, where time-out takes a holiday. While this sounds funny, this inconsistency happens in homes across America all the time (not the Thursday part). I've been there.

Every Single Time is Better, Just Ask Rusty Clark!

At the heart of this zeal for consistency is an understanding of what happens when people are less than consistent. The behavioral contingency loses its ability to produce a change in the target behavior. This is exemplified in a 1973 study conducted at the University of Kansas by Dr. Hewitt "Rusty" Clark and colleagues (Clark, Rowbury, Baer, & Baer, 1973). An 8-year-old child with mental retardation was attending a special school program. This child engaged in a variety of disruptive and aggressive behaviors involving inappropriate physical contact with the other children in the class. The child would bear hug other children, choke them, hit and kick them, and hit objects. Obviously she had not read the book, *How to make friends and influence people*.

When the teacher just ignored the behavior (staff intervened when it looked like she might hurt another child), high rates of disruptive and aggressive behaviors resulted. For 3 days, using this plan, her rate of these behaviors exceeded 20, with a high of 74 occurrences on one day! Simply attending to her for behavior other than inappropriate contact did not produce the desired result in this case. (*Note to reader: Ignoring behavior does not always work as some experts may have led you to believe.*) Dr. Clark and his colleagues then taught the teacher how to use time-out whenever these aggressive behaviors toward other children or objects occurred.

These researchers were interested in ascertaining what happens when time-out is inevitable versus when it is less consistent. Therefore, in one condition, time-out occurred every single time. Let's term that the "inevitable condition". In another condition, these behaviors did not produce a time-out every single time. Rather, time-out occurred once every eight times on the average, this is called a "variable ratio eight (VR 8)" schedule. Sometimes time-out may have occurred on the third occurrence of the aggressive behavior, other times the child may have engaged in aggressive behavior 12 times before the teacher gave her a time-out.

What were the results? The average rate of aggressive behaviors for the inevitable condition was three per day, down from 20 in the previous "ignore it and it will go away" condition. Equally impressive was that in 6 of the 8 days in this inevitable consequence condition, the rate of occurrence of target behaviors was either 0 or 1. In contrast, the average rate of aggressive behaviors for the VR 8 condition was 14 per day. While an intermittent use of time-out was apparently better than no time-out at all, it did not really bring the behavior down to a manageable level. What did work with this girl is the inevitable consequence of aggression being time-out. I have found similar results to Dr. Clark's research in a study we conducted with a child testing two punishing stimuli (Cipani, Brendlinger, Mc Dowell, & Usher, 1991).

The more likely the target behavior produces the intended consequence, the more likely a punishment effect will be achieved. On the other hand, failure to follow through, for whatever reason, lessens the chance of success. But sometimes, consistency requires a lot of effort on the part of the parent. The example below illustrates the amount of effort needed in extreme cases.

The Case of the Future "WWE" Star:
The Price of Persistence

There is certainly much controversy over the imitation of wrestling moves, as observed on TV, by young children. Some children apparently discriminate between what is seen on TV and what is allowed on the playground, but others do not. If a child has a developmental delay, this distinction between TV and real life may be even more clouded.

Such was the case with Barry. He lived with his mother and her common law spouse, Barry's stepfather. Cartoons did not interest him. But when he would hear on TV, "Let's get ready to rumble," he was fixated on the TV. Barry became quite adept at imitating these moves. At first, his target was his stepfather and he readily responded, by play wrestling with his son. However, it became problematic when it occurred with mom, and then his sister. She would try to explain to him how it was inappropriate, and that he cannot always do what he wants. She always stated that she loved him, but she would draw the line when he put her in a full nelson. She tried time-out but reported it did not work (use of unknown proportion to occurrence of aggression). She would occasionally spank him, as a last resort. As my behavioral specialist found out later, she probably did not resort to time-outs very often because of their immediate effect: full scale aggression toward her from Barry.

Our approach was two-fold. We felt that Barry and his stepfather should bond in some fashion and they both seemed to enjoy this play wrestling. The problem was that it extended to other inappropriate times, places, and people. Therefore, we decided to allow it to occur to very limited conditions. The stepfather would play wrestle with him in the living room when he signaled to Barry the advent of the wrestling match. Lastly, a carpet rug used especially for wrestling with his stepfather was advocated, to really make the distinction with Barry.

But Barry was also aggressive when it was to his advantage to be so. For example, his mother might have asked him to pick up something. He may not have wanted to be interrupted in whatever he was doing. If she pressed the issue, she then experienced the "Barry retaliatory" response. We felt that aggression under situations where it was not part of the father-son bonding activity required a time-out. My behavioral specialist trained Barry's mom to deliver the time-out. She escorted him to time-out in a gentle but firm manner, required him to stay there for a continuous period of time, and provided close supervision while he remained in time-out. Getting up from time-out resulted in Barry being put back in time-out by his mother, with an additional amount of time required. Once he quieted down for 30 seconds he was released from time-out.

Barry did not take this new way of handling him in stride. He escalated his assaultive behavior on his mother, as well as physically assaulting property, while being taken to time-out. He continued his rampage while in time-out. This escalation necessitated our teaching Barry's mother how to restrain him when he escalated to this level. We have a saying, "When the going gets tough, are you?"

Many parents who profess that time-out does not work with their young child often give up during these circumstances. Barry's mom was not one of them. She was relentless in her pursuit to enforce the time-out. It was essential that she succeed now when he was only 4 years old. What would happen in a few years when he is bigger and stronger?

Time-out and other additional reinforcement procedures worked well, in drastically reducing aggressive behavior. His rate of tantrums was less frequent and less severe. Additionally, due to a compliance plan, he was now following requests to pick up things by his mother. Eight months after our initial involvement, Barry had learned that there was a time and a place for wrestling. Further, he was not using his tactical knowledge of aggressive moves as an instrument of resistance to parental requests. Barry's mother reported that he still required time-outs for occasional aggressive behavior. However, she was now able to effect the time-out without generating aggressive behavior on Barry's part. He did his time-out without much fuss and then proceeded with the rest of his day. This result is crucial, since Barry was getting physically more capable with age. It was necessary for him to accept consequences for his behavior, while he was still young. Consistency was essential in this case, and it paid off in big dividends.

- Why did the time-out procedure work?
- Are all parents equally capable of effecting time out? If not, should another procedure be considered?

Is the Principle of Consistency Necessary?

Yes, for the reasons illustrated above. I believe that many of the conclusions about punishment are based on applications that have little integrity, as far as consistency goes. For example, Dr. Murray Strauss (1994) concluded in a book that spanking does not work. What research evidence did he use to support his contention? He conducted a study on spanking by asking 270 college students to first identify the year they experienced the most corporal punishment. In other words they were to recollect this information from memory. The mean age, reported by these interviewees, at which the greatest amount of spankings occurred was when they were 8 years old. The average number of spankings reported for that year was six. The college students were then asked what percentage of the time they thought it was effective.

How does the principle of inevitability analyze this result? If the average number of spankings from recall was about six, how consistently do you think spanking was applied for a specific target misbehavior over a year's time period? I know I misbehaved more than six times when I was 8 years old. Six times might have covered 1 week's worth of misbehavior for me. What about the other 51 weeks of the year? Also consider this: My parents and teachers considered me a well-behaved child.

Let's construct hypothetical data to exemplify this argument. Let's say, for argument sake, that some of these people were spanked when they yelled at their mother. If they yelled at their mother about twice a week, on average, how many times over a year would that sum to? About 104, give or take some. Now, these people reported that they were spanked six times. Therefore, roughly 6% of the time they would yell at their mother, they got spanked. That is not even close to being consistent. Any approach that is used 6% of the time is probably not going to succeed. With this type of speculative analysis, can you see why you should not conclude spanking is ineffective from the Strauss data? We just do not know enough at this time to conclude whether spanking works.

How Important is the Immediacy of the Consequence?

A behavioral contingency specifies that a behavior is followed in close temporal proximity by a consequence. How close is close? For many children, telling them that they earned a point, or lost a point, when the behavior occurs, works well. With language, humans are able to bridge the gap between when a behavior occurs and when the consequence is invoked. The child may not get to have extra free time until later that afternoon when he has earned all his points, but such an arrangement still maintains his low levels of target behavior. In this case, the verbal instruction, " you earned points" (or lost points) serves as a bridge to the eventual delivery or lack thereof, and is called a conditioned reinforcer (or conditioned punisher).

The younger the child, the less likely such verbal instructions will be able to bridge the gap. Children with developmental delays may also need consequences that occur in close proximity to the target behavior in order for the behavior to decrease in frequency. Particularly when dealing with young children, the consequence may have to occur at the initial part of the chain of events that comprises the target behavior. For example, a 2-year-old plays close to a curtain and begins tugging on it. If the parent catches the child after he has pulled on it 5-10 times, which is too late (in my clinical experience). Whatever pleasure the child has derived from pulling on the curtains has probably already occurred. One can rest assured that the next time the opportunity presents itself, the child will not feel any inhibition whatsoever to go and pull on the curtain.

In order to make a punishing consequence effective, the parent would need to be more vigilant than he currently is, and catch the child right as she touches the curtain. Better yet, pair a warning (e.g., "Don't touch!") with the delivery of the punisher as she touches the curtain. Once the punishing event has reduced the behavior, the warning can be given before she touches the curtain. The parent gives the warning right when his daughter is in the vicinity, looking at the curtain and thinking how wondrous it would be to touch the curtain. If the warning does not inhibit the grabbing of the curtains, and she touches the curtain, the consequence needs to be applied as before. However, it is essential in some cases to catch the early parts of the chain, as this research study described attests to.

An Effective Immediate Consequence Solves a Life-threatening Problem.

Some infants develop serious, medical, life threatening conditions as a result of rumination. Rumination is the regurgitation of food or liquid (once swallowed) and subsequent ejection of such from the mouth. If such behavior produces significant loss of food intake over a period of time, dehydration, malnutrition and lowered resistance to diseases can occur.

A 6-month old infant was brought to the University of Mississippi Hospital in February of 1972, for failing to gain weight for a second time in her short life because of persistent rumination (Sajwaj, Libet, & Agras, 1974). The presenting problem consisted of the following scenario. Upon being fed milk, Sandra would begin a chain of behaviors, starting with forward and backward tongue thrusting, which resulted in the milk being brought back into the mouth area. From there it would flow out for about a 10-20 minute period, at which time there appeared to be no milk left from the original feeding. It was important for these researchers to analyze all parts of the chain of events that resulted in regurgitation of the milk. Intervening with a punisher once the milk started spilling out of the child's mouth would have probably been too late. The early part of the rumination scenario would have to be halted via the delivery of a powerful contingent event.

Following a baseline assessment of the percentage of time Sandra was engaged in rumination following a feeding, a contingent procedure called lemon juice therapy was administered. (*Note to reader: Not something to be tried at home by novices.*) As soon as the vigorous tongue movements began, 16 cc of unsweetened lemon juice was immediately squirted into her mouth with a syringe. This consequent event was applied each time the tongue thrusting occurred by nursing staff under supervision. A second application was administered if tongue thrusting persisted after a 30-60 second period elapsed (to avoid lip smacking from the sour sensation of the lemon).

The baseline analysis revealed that rumination was occurring at a rate of 40-70% of the time in a 20-minute period following a feeding. Again, this typically led to a loss of all the milk initially swallowed during the feeding. In the first session in which lemon juice was applied, 12 injections of lemon juice were administered. Over the next 15 feedings, the number of applications of the contingent lemon juice was between one and six.

The rate of rumination decreased remarkably. By day 12, no more milk was observed in the mouth, only occasional tongue thrusting (but not followed by regurgitation of milk). By day 23, the percentage of ruminative behavior was either zero or near zero. The desired effect of decreasing rumination on Sandra's health was obtained. Sandra's weight increased and she was discharged back to her foster parents. A 1-year follow-up of her progress put her weight at the 25th percentile for infant girls.

What is the Effectiveness of a Punisher if One Can Escape It?

Another related point to the consistency principle is the delivery of the contingency in its intended fashion. For example, if you designate the removal of TV privileges as a consequence for failing to do homework, are you able to carry this out to its full extent? Or do mitigating conditions arise which frequently have you "giving in" after 15 minutes? If this happens often enough, do you think that the rate of doing homework will be changed for the better? The answer is intuitive, but there are studies that prove the point.

Dr. Nathan Azrin and colleagues empirically demonstrated what happens when you allow the subject to escape the punishing consequence (Azrin, Hake, Holz, & Hutchinson, 1965). In the first part of the experiment, the researchers taught pigeons to peck at a select key. Subsequently, they began punishing the key peck response, and obtained a marked decrease in pecking that key. In the next phase of the experiment, the bird was then allowed to press a second key. Pecking this key resulted in the pigeon getting out of that situation in which key pecks were punished. In very little time, the birds pressed the escape key frequently (imagine that!) after pressing the first key to get food. Of course, the effect of the punishing consequence on pecking the first key is negligible.

Escaping punishment and therefore mitigating its effectiveness to decrease behavior can take on unusual forms in both the animal and human realm. In experiments with rats, shock is delivered to the foot of the rat each time it presses the bar. In order for the shock to occur, the feet apparently have to be on the grid of the floor. I never ran these kinds of experiments when I was in school so I am surmising this from the written study. One particular rat must have had a genetic gift for adapting to severe conditions. This rat would lie down and press the bar from underneath, so that it would not have its feet to the grid. This clever manner of pressing the bar thereby avoided the shock that came with bar pressing. There is a picture of this animal in a book (Fantino & Logan, 1979), and it is entitled "breakfast in bed." You may have to see the picture to appreciate the humor. Anyway, the contingent shock did nothing to eliminate this rat's bar pressing. Organisms are clever! Where there is a will to escape, there is often a way.

What is the human analogue to unauthorized escape from the punishing event? How about kids who say they are sorry, and the time-out is concluded by the parent ("Well, they said they were sorry, and I believe them"). How about kids who cry during time-out? Have you ever wondered why they cry when they are placed in time-out? I don't believe that time-out encompasses any painful intrusive physical stimulus. It is not like they are sitting on hot coals. Put two and two together. If they are eventually taken out upon crying (could be 30 seconds one time, 2 minutes the next), what do you think they have stored in their little neurons as relevant information when in time-out? The rule: If you want to get out of time-out, cry longer and harder. You now see how real life develops rules about what behaviors escape punishing conditions.

What effect does the inability to implement the consequence in the intended fashion have on the target child behavior? The inability to fully implement the punishing consequence would most probably weaken its effect, potentially rendering it ineffective. Many people who claim to have used a consequence allow the child to escape it, usually with a certain level of pleading, whining, and other really undesirable escape-motivated behaviors. After all, how many children have actually been grounded till Christmas?

Principle III: The "Even Swap" Rule

The principle of the "even swap" involves the complimentary use of reinforcement for some desirable behavior in conjunction with the use of a punishing consequence for the target undesirable behavior. In many behavior analysis classes at the undergraduate and graduate level, professors extol the need to include positive reinforcement for some alternate behavior as well as punishment contingencies for the problem behavior. While this again seems intuitive, it may not be practiced in applied settings.

Upon being granted my Ph.D. from Florida State University in 1979, I worked on a unit of a state institution in Wisconsin for persons with disabilities. One day in the beginning of my tenure, I came upon a client engaging in self- injury while several staff sat back and appeared to be practicing relaxation techniques. I felt that there should be some action on their part, and was amazed that they did not feel compelled to remotely look like they were intervening in some way. This tells you how much influence I had at the time.

After awhile, when it was evident that this was apparently standard operating procedure, I asked them, "What behavioral plan has been developed for this individual's self-injury?" They remarked, "Oh, we are ignoring him so that he will stop doing that. You know, ignoring the behavior to make it go away." Well there you have it. There was a good explanation for what I observed. "Ok, I can see that. And you are doing a fine job of ignoring that behavior as well as anything else he does. If ignoring works the way you say it does, why in no time at all, he will be void of any behavior. Why, with the adroit skill with which you are ignoring him, he may eventually return to an amoeba, a single cell state. Keep up the good work."

Look What Happened in the Laboratory— Combining Reinforcement with Punishment.

Sarcasm aside, complementing punishment with reinforcement is not just a catchy phrase. Researchers at Anna State Hospital examined this principle by measuring the key peck behavior of pigeons under two different circumstances (Holz & Azrin, 1963). The first condition was similar to many other studies. Once the key peck response was established by food reinforcement, punishment via shock was delivered for key pecks. These procedures test how well punishment will inhibit a behavior that has already been developed under reinforcement. Under this condition, three birds had the following average rates (across multiple sessions) of key peck responses respectively: 3, 23, and 93 (that last bird- talk about failing to profit from experience).

In the second condition, using other pigeons, the same key resulted in punishment. However, another key was made available which resulted in food for key pecks, but no punishment for pecking it. The rate of key pecks to the key that resulted in punishment dropped dramatically for all three birds respectively: 0, 0, and 1. Of course this now makes sense. With another venue for obtaining food, one that did not require them to sustain shock, the results make sense.

How Does this Apply to a Parent's Use of Punishing Consequences?

The even swap rule has tremendous implications for parents. The objective to reduce a child's target problem behavior is made more probable if you can combine punishment of a target behavior with reinforcement of an alternate behavior. Unfortunately, too often, parents (and others) jump to the use of a consequence for the target problem behavior. As you will see, it is just as effective, or more so, to decrease a target behavior by building something to take its place. I teach the following to students and parents alike: Every time you want to target a specific undesirable behavior for a decrease, concurrently determine what behavior(s) you want to increase. In this manner, there will be an even swap (i.e., reducing an undesirable behavior while developing an appropriate replacement).

The punishers that involve a removal of reinforcement for target behavior inherently take advantage of reinforcement. For that reason, I highly recommend their use. For example, let us say that a parent wants to target her son's aggressive behavior toward his younger sister. If the behavioral contingency is that the child loses a half an hour off bedtime that night for hitting his sister, he concurrently gains that privilege if he does not hit his sister during the day. Hence reinforcement and punishment are at work, hand in hand. The case below illustrates the even swap principle with a unique problem.

The Case of the Intimate Disclosure

We received a referral for a 21-year-old female, Clarine, with a very unique, but problematic behavior. Clarine had mild mental retardation and lived with foster parents subsequent to her being taken out of her father's home (the reason will be apparent in a minute). She was a fairly capable and pleasant individual and could engage in a variety of tasks that would allow her to gain paid employment with some help. At the time of the referral, she was working at a convalescent hospital and was being trained by any agency to gain and maintain that place of employment.

Her work at the hospital seemed to meet everyone's expectations, but she was to be fired from her job for a reason other than her ability to make a bed. Clarine made friends easily, perhaps too easily. She would initiate a conversation with the patients at the hospital in an appropriate manner (this attention is often a welcome event in these patients lives). However, without a moments notice, she would begin talking with them as if they had been hired as her psychiatrist or social worker. What am I referring to? In mid conversation, she would provide explicit details about her biological father sexually abusing her (in graphic details) as well as a rape that occurred to her when she was in school. The conversation might start with, "Hi, my name is Clarine, what is your name. How are you doing? Do you like it here? Do you want to hear how my father undressed me and *******?"

The staff person who worked with her had tried many strategies to get her to stop disclosing all the intricacies of her unfortunate past, but to no avail. Imagine the reaction you would have if you were a patient in this hospital. Here comes a pleasant individual who wants to make conversation with you. Your agenda is not entirely filled up on this particular day, so you greet her with a smile. The conversation is pleasant and seems to be going along fine and then you do a double take, discounting the possibility that you heard ******. Nope there is nothing wrong with your ears. Your smile turns to a look of apprehension and finally, distaste. As you might guess, Clarine did not pick up on some subtle cues that one's interest had turned to aversion for her story. The patient's attention was all that mattered, and such was being given in abundance for her remarks about her unfortunate past life.

To complicate matters, this probable attention from patients would make it more difficult to eliminate such a behavior. One could not count on this attention to stop in the near future. It would be improbable to get everyone at her work site, as well as visitors to agree to ignore this one worker when she said, "**********." I don't believe the Americans with Disabilities Act would extend that far in terms of a reasonable accommodation. This situation required that we come up with a strategy that would make it more uncomfortable for her to engage in this behavior. Additionally, the planned consequence needs to override the social attention such behavior probably receives.

The administrators at the hospital were adamant about her leaving, and fired her. Luckily another job at a day care was procured by her social worker. My behavioral specialist and I felt that it was essential to have a plan in place that would be so powerful that it would make Clarine think twice before launching into her sermon. Prior to Clarine showing up at her new position, my behavioral specialist worked with the foster parents to teach them how to use evening privileges as a consequent event. If Clarine had an incident at work that day, all evening privileges were revoked. She would basically become bored until she went to sleep that night. Tomorrow was another day when she could keep or lose that evening's privileges.

What would she have to do to lose evening privileges? You guessed it. Each day the supervisor would report to the staff aide helping Clarine about any incident of inappropriate conversation. If any incident occurred, this was conveyed to her parents and privileges were revoked that evening. Conversely, if she kept her conversation in tow, then she did not lose evening privileges. Additionally any chores at work that were assigned, and not completed due to lack of motivation on her part would also result in her evening privileges being revoked.

Apparently this consequence struck fear into Clarine. Not one single major incident of inappropriate disclosure occurred at the day care within the first 2-months. This plan was effective because it provided a powerful consequence for inappropriate disclosure as well as a reinforcing condition if she did not disclose such facts while at work.

This case is instructive for another reason as well. Sometimes a punishing consequence has to be used to override the effects of a powerful social reinforcer that the behavior frequently produces, because people are people! When some people do or say wacky things, other people stand up and take notice, and laugh and attend. Overriding this built-in reinforcement for intimate disclosures required the foster parents to remove preferred events when such occurred. While other people may have felt that Clarine needed to talk about this earlier trauma in her life, my position was that its indiscriminate occurrence was not healthy for anyone. Subsequent to the success of this program, I do not see that Clarine's emotional health suffered because we punished such a disclosure. In fact, Clarine was better for it and I'm sure the day care was also happy with the result.

- Why do you think Clarine engaged in such intimate disclosures with strangers?
- Do you believe the intervention negatively affected Clarine's ability to deal with her past? Why or why not?

Principle IV: Remove Competing Consequences

Figuratively speaking, have you ever dug a hole and then had someone fill it back up? Then you dug the same hole a second time and again to your dismay, found that someone filled it back up? What would be your reaction if you found out that someone was hired to fill up holes you dug, which you were completely unaware of. Of course you would feel like your work was in vain.

The same phenomenon can occur when punishing a behavior. If a child's problem behavior is producing an unintended reinforcer, while a punishing event is being applied, the effect may be minimal. If this exists, it certainly mimics the illustration of the example of the hole digging and subsequent refilling.

The noted behavioral therapist and educator, the late Dr. Glen Latham, was a consultant on a case that illustrates this principle nicely. Everyday, this boy in an elementary school would be sent down to the principal's office for some misbehavior (mistake #1: behavioral contingency missing). The consternation of the school was that his behavior was getting worse, not better. This boy was apparently beyond any intervention known to mankind (since sending him to the principal's office only exacerbated the problem).

Dr. Latham went to visit the school one day early, wanting to see what this young boy did to result in his being sent to the principal's office. From his description, I ventured that the office was the main gateway to the rest of the school. This must have been a heavy traffic area in the morning. Unfortunately, Dr. Latham was too late in arriving that day. This boy was already in the office! In fact, he appeared to have taken on the role of official greeter of the school. Schoolmates, parents, and anyone who went by the office on their way to the classroom passed by him, and he did his best to greet them all. He appeared to be pleased at this form of "punishment." He looked like a kid who was locked in the candy store all night.

On the one hand, getting sent to the office means you will have to meet with a possibly unfriendly principal and lose recess. On the other hand, you get one of the neatest jobs in the school. Do you see the dilemma? One person digs the hole. The other person fills it up.

Often the use of time-out may provide a competing contingency, which wrecks havoc on its ability to effect behavior change. I worked with one child whose mother would send him to time-out in the afternoon. To my objection, he was sent to his bedroom. On one of my visits he had already been sent to his room. When I asked, " Where is John?" the mother told me he was in time-out. "How long has he been there?" Her reply, "About 30 minutes." That long, I thought. Let's go have a look. As she opened the door he was on his bed sleeping. I remarked, "I'll bet he gets time-out every afternoon about this time." Yeah, she replies. He can be really cranky, and act mean to his sister, every afternoon like clockwork." Would you say time-out was working for this child? For inducing sleep, yes. For aggression to sister, no.

Sometimes, parents or staff engineer competing consequences to avoid producing a punishment contingency as the two cases below illustrate.

The Case of: You Cannot Go to the YMCA Because You Hit Someone- So Let's Go Out for Donuts

A 13-year-old male, Barry, was housed in a group home in Central California. Barry was physically big for his age, and had frequent incidents of hitting the other residents. The owner of the facility requested that I set up a "behavior mod" program for him. In addition to aggression to other residents, Barry also was frequently noncompliant to staff requests, which was a common occurrence with many residents in the home. He also had a high rate of swearing, which also seemed to be an entry requirement for residents of the facility.

These behaviors had not improved dramatically. Barry, along with the other residents, had group therapy weekly; group meetings with staff, psychiatric involvement, and a variety of point systems. In the latter case, observation revealed that what consequences were delineated on paper did not often transpire in real life.

In being given the assignment, I went over the records to determine what the rate of hitting other children was over the last several weeks. While there were several incident reports when the victim received some injury, staff noted that the actual rate of aggression was much higher, since aggression that did not result in injury was not recorded. Hence, I found it difficult to ascertain the true level of aggression.

One of the activities Barry and the other residents liked was going to the YMCA. The YMCA had a pool and co-ed swimming. The residents of the facility went three days per week. I asked if Barry, as well as other residents, had to meet any behavioral criterion in order to go. The staff person remarked, "Well he has to be good." I then followed up with the following question, "How many times in the last several weeks did he lose the privilege of going with the group to the YMCA?" Answer: "None." I thought to myself. "Ok, and this is the same kid that hits someone everyday? What is the definition of misbehavior we are using for Barry, maiming or destroying someone?"

It seemed logical to me that we should set some more definitive criteria for this potentially powerful reinforcing activity. The plan I drew up to impede the frequency of aggression toward other residents was the following: An act of aggression toward another resident would remove his upcoming trip to the YMCA. For example, if he aggressed against someone on Tuesday, he would miss the Wednesday evening outing. If he went from Thursday to Saturday without hitting anyone he would then be allowed to go on the Saturday night outing. I explained this to the house staff and the house manager. I was insured that staff would record each offense in writing.

I had expected that this consequence for aggressing against peers would put a huge dent in Barry's proclivity for hitting and punching. My follow-up visit 1-week hence was a huge disappointment. The records showed no real significant change in his aggressive behavior. In fact, he missed all of the scheduled YMCA trips. I was taken aback, and quite frankly did not know why this had not succeeded. Maybe I misjudged his love of the YMCA.

In an inquisitive manner, I asked the staff person, "When Barry misses out on the YMCA outing, he must be a *bear* to keep in the house. What do you do with him?" The answer from the staff came like a beaming light in a dark room: "Oh, we cannot keep him home. He would go berserk and tear up the place. A staff person takes him for donuts, or he goes bowling." Ok, I see what was going on. If Barry did not earn one activity, we apparently provided him with an alternate activity, hopefully one that was equally pleasing. Of course, we avoided at all costs Barry getting upset because the consequence for his aggressive behavior was not to his liking. Let us try to give him a consequence for aggression that is something he will be relatively happy with.

If you ever wondered why behavioral plans don't work, consider this a primary example of what goes on when things don't work. If I had not asked some questions, I might have been under the assumption that this plan was ineffective in its design. No, the plan was not at fault here. The staff expertly engineered a strong competing contingency.

- Why did loss of YMCA activities as a consequence for aggression not work in Barry's case?
- How would you handle this problem?

He Likes to Be Restrained!

In the mid-1980s I was hired as a consultant for a training program for people with developmental disabilities. The staff wanted me to assess clients who had severe behavior problems, including aggression to staff and other clients. It was not uncommon for a client to have to be physically restrained as a result of his (or her) behavior being potentially dangerous to self or others. The restraint would occur at a point where the client's behavior had escalated so that danger was imminent. The staff were well-trained in this procedure and executed it in a safe and efficient manner when needed. While some clients only needed to be restrained every once in awhile, others were restrained daily.

One client in particular was brought to my attention. His rate of behavioral episodes where he had to be restrained was quite high. Why would someone do something that results reliably in restraint? The staff reasoned that restraint should always function as a punisher, since no one in their right mind could actually like this. Therefore the staff's contention was that his behavior was unpredictable, and probably the result of just "going off." In the eyes of the staff, there was no alternative except to restrain him. I thought, "Could there be a competing consequence? What could he possibly be getting out of the restraint process, so that getting this event would override the aversive aspect of the restraint?" The answer? Coffee.

As reported by staff, he would be restrained when his state of aggressive behavior reached the danger point. Two or more staff persons would put him in a prone containment in a safe manner, preferably to a soft surface. As he calmed down, they began a process of releasing him progressively, until he was standing erect again. They would then have him sit in a chair to calm down further, where he was giving lots of attention from staff, soothing comments and coffee. The proof that coffee was the smoking gun was the following piece of information I obtained. Prior to the incident, if he asked for coffee, he would have been told he could not have any till lunch since he just had some for breakfast. Now do you see the competing consequences? Act up, get restrained, then 15-20 minutes later, you get coffee. Don't act up, but ask nicely, you get no coffee. Do you see the choice?

Principle V: Be Specific

I once read a report for a child, with a recommendation for treating his behavior problems as the following. "When he engages in good behavior, reinforce him. Of course when he engages in misbehavior, you should not reward him." Thank you for that! Such words of wisdom are certainly worth the $130/hour fee rate from whoever provided that consultation. It is obvious that only someone with advanced graduate training would have been able to produce such an insightful recommendation! Clearly, their graduate training program did a fine job in teaching this mental health professional all she or he needs to know about using consequences.

While this example is quite extreme, it often is the case that the exact nature of the punishing consequence is not specified. For example, a recommendation such as "ignore the behavior" does not constitute precise consequences. How long should one ignore? What should one do when engaged in ignoring?

In the study cited earlier by Dr. Agras and colleagues (Sajwaj, et.al., 1974) the consequence of rumination was precisely specified (i.e., 16 cc of lemon juice squirted into the client's mouth with a syringe). Each application should not have varied that specification. This punishing consequence is precisely specified so that it will be administered in the same fashion each time. If you decide to use certain procedures to effect change in your child's behavior, it is imperative that you adhere to this principle. The specification of the consequence should be delineated before initiating the strategy. Do not fly by the seat of your pants, you will probably end up without pants!

Some available instruments make specification more reasonable for everyday use of consequences. I have often used a portable oven timer when measuring the length of time-out. The number of times a child must correct some behavior as a consequence can be delineated (e.g., if you fail to put the towel on the rack, you must practice this 10 times before eating lunch). Perhaps there is a necessary balance between the rigor required and obtained in research studies and the applications of parental consequences in Merritt Island, Florida. We may not get precision to the nth degree, but let's avoid ambiguity to the 5th exponent.

Principle VI: Prove It Works

The development of basic principles of punishment were formulated from years of research in animal laboratories before such procedures were used with children, adolescents, and adults. Research findings have driven application and theory. We do not have a theory regarding which events will always function as a punisher. For example, claiming that spanking is necessary for child development because it teaches children right from wrong, is not something that can be proven across the board (see example below). On the other hand, we also do not advocate that ignoring a behavior will always be the best approach for parents to use in teaching their child to avoid certain patterns of behavior. When you hear that, it is not science, it is dogma. Punishment and reinforcement contingencies are determined in each individual situation. One cannot simply be a time-out expert and be reliably effective in dealing with child problem behaviors.

The field of behavior analysis has taken the same basic track as other sciences. The technology developed was the result of many studies conducted by experimental and applied researchers over a 6-decade history. Rather than adopting unwavering loyalty to some manner of dealing with child behavior, testing of effective procedures became the field's mainstay. The practical use of these procedures occurred once there was sufficient evidence that a behavioral effect was reliably obtained in several studies.

One should take heart in the progression of the application of behavioral principles from the early laboratory developments investigating the science of behavior. There is no need to apologize anymore for the use of techniques derived from laboratory research conducted decades ago. If anything, the general populace should be encouraged by this track. The apology should be forthcoming from approaches that have no empirical basis whatsoever, yet have run out to sell their "therapy wares" to the market!

This rich history of findings about reinforcement and punishment effects in the laboratory, led to the application of these principles to help people with real life problems. Given the lineage of applied researchers in the 1950s and 1960s, there was an insistence on validating clinical procedures with real life problems before mass marketing. One study would verify that some procedure had an effect on five children with disruptive levels of behavior. Then someone would conduct another study that used other children, with a different set of behaviors, verifying the effectiveness of that same procedure. The replication of successful results occurred many times over before a procedure was granted empirical verification status. Below are research examples of such empirical verification.

Medication is Not Always the Answer: Time-out Does Work.

A 4-year-old child, Brian, who was diagnosed with emotional disturbance and mental retardation, attended a special school for children with these disorders at the University of Washington (Shafto & Sulzbacher, 1977). Brian was often observed wandering aimlessly about the classroom. One of the major problems reported by staff was that he engaged in frequent activity changes (operational definition of hyperactive behavior in this case). During the baseline condition, Brian's frequency of activity changes was simply recorded, with no special intervention occurring.

Following a first baseline condition of 20 days, Brian was given 5 mg. of Ritalin, twice daily, for four sessions. Again the rate of activity changes was accurately measured to assess the effects of this intervention in contrast to baseline. On the fifth session, the teacher added a behavioral component to the medication intervention for another 11 days. The teacher attended to him when he was engaged in appropriate play, as well as provided cereal reinforcement for staying with the toy or play activity. The consequence for moving to another area before spending significant time with the current toy or activity was the withdrawal of attention and food reinforcement.

How did that work? The medication combined with the behavioral strategy produced substantial changes in child behavior. To demonstrate that the treatment was the critical factor for the change of behavior, the researchers removed the treatment. Guess what result that produced? When the medication and behavioral contingency were removed, Brian went back to changing the play activity frequently.

What would Brian do if medication alone was used? In the next condition, a comparison between 5 mg and 15 mg of Ritalin was assessed. Either dosage level did not decrease his activity-changing behavior substantially from the prior baseline. The article reported that the mother requested that the medication intervention be terminated earlier than desired by the researchers. Brian's mother was not happy with his staying awake at night later and later. Following that abrupt change in plans, the behavioral contingency was reinstituted. A return to behavioral intervention resulted in a decrease of activity changes, without any medication being given during this time period.

In the above study, we know what caused the decrease in activity changes. It was the behavioral contingency. Correlation studies do not allow for this cause and effect analysis, despite many an author's insistence on claiming such. Not all research studies are equally credible in concluding cause and effect.

Need Positive Practice at Staying in Your Seat (During Recess Time)?

A unique application of a behavioral contingency termed positive practice was used for a 9-year-old student, Herbie. Herbie was fine when he was in his seat. However, when he got out of his seat, it was apparently not a quiet event. He was disruptive, loud, aggressive to other third-grade children, and non-compliant. As a result of these behaviors both his academic performance as well as his relationships with the other children in the class deteriorated. Researchers at the University of Montana, under the direction of Dr. Phillip Bornstein, were involved to help the third-grade teacher with Herbie's behavior (Bornstein, Hamilton, & Quevillon, 1977).

The punishment contingency involved the following for each occurrence of out-of-seat behavior. First, Herbie was immediately informed that he had broken the rule (about staying in one's seat). Second, each infraction cost him three minutes at noon (during recess time) to practice appropriate behavior. During that recess period, he had to: (1) recite the following rule, "do not get out of your seat without permission and (2) perform the following; raise your hand and upon being acknowledged by the teacher, ask permission to leave the seat.

What should happen if Herbie refused to perform the practice regimen at recess? These researchers also devised a unique way of dealing with any thoughts by this child to defeat the plan. Herbie's refusal had an additional consequence: additional time would be added for practice (meaning less time for noon recess). That additional contingency was apparently very effective in shutting down the possibility of refusing to engage in the practice regimen. Refusal only happened twice during the entire program.

The results showed the superiority of this punishment procedure over simply reminding Herbie about the rules. By the third day of this program, Herbie's rate of out-of-seat behavior dwindled from an average rate of 20 (when the teacher just stated the rules to him) to less than 5. This study was important because it contrasts the differential results obtained under punishment versus other approaches. Another test condition that proved ineffective was based on a counseling approach. The teacher was told that he should deal with the "real inner problem" in order to get Herbie to stay in his seat. In other words, talk to him and see what is the problem. While no one can say for sure how much "deep psychological analysis" went on, whatever transpired did not do much for Herbie's out-of-seat behavior. Getting to Herbie's inner thoughts, without positive practice consequences, had a deleterious effect on out-of-seat instances. The average rate jumped back to an unacceptable level; 18 daily occurrences during this period.

While the rate of out-of-seat behavior during the punishment condition was markedly lower than it was during the other two test conditions, it was not yet at zero. That was taken care of by adding a nice bonus (i.e., supplementing reinforcement with punishment) to the program. Herbie had to count accurately his out-of-seat behavior for the morning. If he was within one of the teacher's count, he earned a bonus of 15 extra recess minutes. This double edge contingency resulted in great improvements, with about 50 days of 0 or 1 instance of out-of-seat behavior for the day. From 20 per day to 0 per day is success, of which there can be no argument. Mention this study the next time someone says tells you that getting children to understand why they behave in a certain manner is all that is needed. It would be nice if that were all one needed to do to change child behavior. But unlike the inhabitants on Freudania, we live on planet Earth.

Section IV:
A Responsible Use of Punishment

It should now be clear that understanding what constitutes punishment and how it produces changes in child behavior can make you a more effective parent. All children, at one time or another, engage in behaviors that are undesirable. Using consequences (both reinforcement and punishment) effectively can make such behaviors not become a reliable pattern in children's dealings with their environment. Further, many effective punishing consequences can entail the removal of reinforcement, without resorting to physical means of consequating behavior. But the use of consequences has more far reaching ramifications.

I believe that part of becoming a well-functioning adult is based on an individual's ability to endure unpleasant events and consequences. Unpleasant events are part of everyday life. In some unfortunate circumstances, unpleasant events are not even contingent upon one's behavior (e.g., sickness or death of a family member or friend). One of my colleagues, Dr. Merrill Winston from Florida, made a clever analysis of life one night at a conference social event. (*Note to reader: I did not inquire if he does his best thinking with an adult beverage or two in his system.*) He remarked something along the following lines, "Our ability as a species to profit from punishing events and bring our behavior in accordance with such contingencies is a testament to our survival." That might well be the mantra for this book! If we are unable to profit from experiencing unwanted consequences, what would be our fate? If we do not learn to dress warmly in environments where the temperature gets below zero, how long can we survive? It is important for us to learn to adjust our behavior as a function of unwanted consequences.

Let me preach for just a minute. It is our job, our obligation, as parents, to teach our children how to behave in a manner that recruits social reinforcement. But I think this is achieved only when children are accustomed to accepting consequences for their behavior. Therefore, it is necessary to teach your child how to accept minimally to moderate unpleasant consequences, as part of growing up. As children get older, the consequences for behavior become more unpleasant, even though such consequences are not painful in any physical sense. If not making the little league baseball team as a result of striking out during try-outs is tough to handle, it may pale in comparison to losing one's job when you have four other people depending on you.

The ability to accept consequences for one's behavior, in a manner that does not provoke the social environment to "pile on" additional consequences determines a child's adaptability to the social environment. People who exacerbate their level of undesirable behavior often make things worse for themselves in the long run. *Learning to accept consequences as a child, I believe, leads one to develop as a stronger, emotionally-stable, adult.*

As adults many of us have learned that we cannot always get our way. The difference between successful adulthood and the opposite is the ability to competently handle (in an emotional sense) life's unpleasant circumstances. Dr. Dan Goleman wrote extensively about such in his groundbreaking book (Goleman, 1995). I believe emotional intelligence is determined, to a large degree, by an individual's ability to behave in an appropriate manner in the face of unpleasant or unwanted consequences.

I have cited many cases in this book of children who not only improved their behavior, but also improved their acceptance of consequences for undesirable behavior. Their initial reaction to such consequences was often one of disdain for their parents or teachers. Some children initially displayed more severe reactions to imposed consequences, such as tantrums, screaming bouts, and aggression. However, almost all these children by the end of the intervention period not only behaved more appropriately (to avoid punishment), but also learned how to accept such consequences for their undesirable behavior. As parents, our objective is to teach our children how to *face the music* (both the good and the bad). In my opinion, providing consequences for undesirable behavior, from an early age, is the best vehicle for accomplishing that objective.

Before delineating a model for using punishment responsibly and effectively, a caveat is in order. I am not implying that everyone who reads this material should now deploy punishing consequences. In some cases, a child's behavior may require more than just a do-it-yourself approach. In these circumstances, it is best to get the aide of an expert in applied behavior analysis. This person can consult with the parent and provide help in the design and implementation of the strategy. To learn more about these professionals, go to www.bacb.com. For professionals wanting additional information and training on behavioral practice, I have developed a 22-hour certificate program that is available on the internet. Go to *www.alliant.edu/ce/online/cipani*.

To entertain whether you are ready to responsibly use punishment contingencies as an adjunct to reinforcement, ask yourself the following questions:

Am I Willing to Solve One Problem Behavior at a Time?

Can you resist the temptation to solve all of your child's problems in one felt swoop? A responsible use of punishing consequences entails the selection of one target behavior from a host of problems, and deploys the punishing consequence for that behavior only. Both the research studies as well as the case examples I have presented illustrated this judicious use of a punishing consequence. Let us examine the case of Barry, the future WWE wrestler. Was time-out used for all problem behaviors? No! Its use was specific to aggressive behavior. It might have been tempting to address his many behavioral problems with time-out, but that probably would have been disastrous. How consistent would Barry's mother have been if she had to deploy time-out for multiple behaviors? Instead of 1 to 3 time-outs per day, she would have had to deploy time-out 20 to 30 times per day. Can you see where time-out will lose its potency?

Similarly with the case of aggressive behavior at Head Start, only aggressive behavior on the playground resulted in time-out. Certainly there were other problem behaviors that occurred on the playground (e.g., not coming in from recess in a timely manner). However, using time-out as the contingency for the myriad of behaviors on the playground would have probably led to inconsistent implementation of time-out, thus gaining nothing.

Take the necessary time to incrementally change your child's host of problem behaviors. As my mother used to say, "Rome was not built in a day." It may take awhile for you to build your Rome, but believe me, the wait is well worth it. If you are willing to decide a priori what the consequence will be for a specific behavior, you have taken your first step toward a responsible use of punishment.

Am I Willing to Deploy That Consequence Consistently?

Do you commit to consistency in the application of punishment consequences? The toughest part of changing child behavior is the continuity needed in responding to every instance of the target behavior. Unfortunately, children do not engage in the target behavior only when you are ready (physically, emotionally and intellectually) to deal with them. They can misbehave when you are at your lowest level of energy. Everyone professes to be consistent. Will your actions back up your words?

In the case of Clarine, the inappropriate discloser, think of what a different outcome might have been generated if her parents or the staff person were inconsistent. Suppose the staff person who recorded her target inappropriate disclosures had decided to sometimes let Clarine off with a warning? What do you think she might have learned from this inconsistency? Clarine might have come away with the following, "Sometimes I lose privileges when I talk about these events to people at my job site, and sometimes I don't." It is important to remember that in this case, these inappropriate statements are unfortunately producing a reinforcer, attention from people. It was essential that the staff person assigned to work with Clarine in her job-training program counted every instance of the target behavior. It was also essential that the parents deployed the intended consequence for inappropriate disclosures when they occurred. The real heroes of this change in Clarine's behavior were the staff person and Clarine's foster parents. Without their commitment to inevitable consequences, Clarine would not have lasted long on her new job. And that would be unfortunate, for both her self-esteem and social life. This plan taught Clarine that one could have a job and friends without having to disclose every intimate detail of one's life.

Am I Willing to Sit Down and Think Through a Plan Before Putting Anything into Action?

Everyone wants to be a "Johnny-on-the-spot," problem solver. Unfortunately most people cannot effectively solve problems when the child is screaming because she wants the "fun meal," instead of the regular hamburger. Some parents solve this crisis by giving the child the fun meal, once the screaming has reached major proportions. Others threaten to take action but do not follow through with consequences.

Many of these child behavioral incidents repeat themselves over and over. While you may be caught off guard with the first screaming bout in the fast food restaurant, what is your excuse when this has occurred repeatedly for two months? Sit down, once you are away from the crisis situation, and work out a plan that deals with the behavior. When screaming occurs the next time, you have already determined what to do.

Am I Willing to Complement Punishment with Reinforcement?

Many of the cases I have presented in this book as well as the research studies have demonstrated that a physically punishing consequence is not usually necessary to change child behavior. Remember Jerry, the case where his mother tied him to a chair because she did not know what else to do? A natural inclination of some parents would be to spank Jerry when his behavior reached that intolerable level. But spanking was unnecessary. His mother's use of the sit and decide technique, combined with a reinforcement plan for increasing his compliance to parental requests worked extremely well.

It is easy for some people to resort to a physically punishing consequence on the spur of the moment. I believe that too many things can go wrong when parents rely solely on spanking as a consequence for misbehavior. Antonio presented a mountain of problems. Can you imagine what problems might have occurred if the plan was for the grandmother to spank Antonio for arguing with his sister? Teaching his grandmother the use of contingent bedtime resulted in substantial changes, without her needing to physically spank him.

I want to add another imperative for you in deciding on a system of consequences for your child. Take it upon yourself to learn all you can about the power of positive reinforcement and behavioral skill training plans. While this material has focused on punishing consequences and some of the myths perpetrated about punishment, do not take this as an indication of my sole use of such. To be an effective parent, you must spend time learning what advances the field of applied behavior analysis has made with respect to building new behaviors in people's repertoires. While I cannot go into great detail on these advancements, since appropriate treatment of this topic would require an entire book, let it be known that knowledge in this area is paramount. Become an enthusiastic consumer of behavior analysis methods. A good place to start is the web site *www.bacb.com*.

Am I Willing to Specify Precisely the Punishing Consequence for the Target Behavior?

The specification of the length of the time-out period should not be, "until he has had enough." Specify where the time-out area will be located, how long the child will remain there, and what the child will be required to do in order to be removed from time-out.

Similarly, if the removal of a privilege is to be the consequence, establish when the privilege is to be given (or not given), the length of time the privilege is in effect, and what the alternate activity is if the privilege is not earned. "Until hell freezes over," is an unacceptable description of the length of time the child loses the privilege.

Am I Willing to Evaluate the Punisher's Effectiveness on the Target Behavior?

Determining the effectiveness of a behavioral plan requires the collection of data every day. This adherence to the collection of data on the target behavior can often seem overzealous and nonessential to some. But it is the hallmark of effective intervention.

It is often difficult for parents to collect data on the daily rate of the target behaviors. However, collection of data is essential to avoid making capricious decisions about the effectiveness of a behavioral plan. When you change a plan, or consider it to be ineffective, you should not do this on the basis of an emotional crisis that is currently facing you. Crises can overwhelm your sense of judgment and appreciation of the successful history of the plan. Responding with changes in the designated plan with each new crisis leads to implementing a new plan frequently. Each new plan is judged ineffective with the next crisis. Pretty soon, you run out of plans.

Review your child's progress on the target behaviors periodically. Let the child's level of progress guide you in your decision to continue (or not continue) the plan.

Am I Willing to Persist Long Enough?

Too many people throw in the towel too early. Consequences do not usually work with just two applications. Keep in mind that we are not changing hair color, we are changing child behavior of long-standing nature.

Are you willing to persist beyond the possible escalation of a child's behavior, to the point of success. If children accepted consequences readily, then everyone's kids would be easy to handle and we would not have a huge commercial market for parenting books! Just because your child makes it difficult for you to remove the privilege does not mean it should be discontinued as a consequence. The efficacy of the punishing consequence is not judged on how well the child likes it. Particularly during difficult times, your persistence is needed.

The cases I have presented in this book exemplify persistence. It was the parents, teachers, and adult care takers who are to be credited with changing behavior. If they were less than resolute in their commitment to change the child's behavior, their story would be like countless others I have worked with (i.e., a non-story or a sad story). It is so often the case that a parent reports that the strategy has not worked, after trying it once or twice. Realize that there is possibly nothing you can do once or twice to change your child's behavior. Your perseverance is the tool needed to develop your child's appropriate behaviors. It's up to you! No one said being a parent is easy, and your resolve will be tested time and time again.

Am I Willing to Be Open to Revising the Plan When It is Ineffective?

On the one hand, you need to persist with a consequence until it demonstrates that it is not going to be effective. However, plans that prove ineffective over a long period of time should be revised. If you are using time-out, and over a period of 4 weeks the target behavior has not decreased even slightly over baseline, alter your plan. There should be no sacred cows. One's preference regarding the use of time-out should not take precedence over the requirement to change the child's problem behavior.

A story told to me by one of my professors illustrates this need for being sensitive to the efficacy of a plan (J. Bailey, personal communication, September, 22, 2002). He was apparently raised on a ranch with horses. His father taught him how to shoe a horse. Basically, the shoe is nailed into the horse's foot, which can obviously create discomfort (on the part of the horse). The person's sensitivity to the horse's response to each hit on the shoe determines whether there will be discomfort to the human performing this delicate operation. Over time young boys in the southwest who become accomplished ranchers learn how to modify their approach to each horse, being sensitive to each horse's response, moment by moment. If you go and whack away, you will not last long in that business. Learn to be sensitive to the data. Treat it as if you are shoeing a horse.

I will end *Punishment on Trial* with a case example. This case illustrates the responsible use of punishing consequences in conjunction with reinforcement of appropriate social behaviors.

Case Study- A Responsible Use of Punishment

Darrian was a 4-year-old boy who was adopted by his paternal grandparents, Felicia and Rinaldo. He had been with his grandparents for more than half a year when I first made contact with this family. I asked Felicia why she was seeking help at the time. Her response was something to this effect, "I can't imagine how a kindergarten or first grade teacher will handle him. I don't think he will get better just by getting older. If my husband and I are hard pressed to deal with his constant misbehaviors day in and day out, what will someone who is not related to him do? I am worried that he will exit himself out of an educational experience because of his behavior, not because he can't learn." Both his grandparents attributed his lack of self-control to his poor upbringing, where little to no consequences were enforced. This certainly seemed plausible from everything I had read or been told of by the adoptions worker.

Darrian presented problems in both home and school environments. He was frequently aggressive to his grandfather, hitting or kicking him with little provocation. He had severe tantrums when he was presented with a situation that did not please him. Felicia relayed a poignant example of this to me. One day on the way to the YMCA preschool program, Felicia picked up her niece (Jodi) to take her to the YMCA as well. When they arrived at school, Felicia opened the door and said, "Let's let Jodi out first." Darrian flew into a rage. He got out of the car and threw himself on the sidewalk, performing bad landscaping on the flowers and plants lining the sidewalk to the YMCA. Felicia got him up off the sidewalk, but Darrian was still in a rage. She quickly ushered him into the class. As you can imagine, an hour later, the YMCA called Felicia and insisted that she take Darrian home because he was uncontrollable. I guess you could say he was suspended from preschool.

Darrian was also rude and aggressive to peers. As a result, very few of his classmates at the YMCA played with him and he had very few friends outside of school. It was reported that he could not play for longer than a few minutes before fighting or name-calling erupted. At school he was also non-compliant to teacher instructions and did not follow school rules. Subsequently he was frequently in trouble and the YMCA preschool was considering his expulsion.

Darrian had numerous problems. Felicia, Rinaldo and I agreed that it was essential to target each of his many problems separately, and not to intervene in too many problems at one time. Rome was not built in a day. Darrian's behavior change would not be either. We decided to target aggression to Rinaldo first. The consequence for aggression was a swiftly implemented time-out. I believed time-out would be perfect for teaching Darrian to engage in playful, appropriate behavior with Rinaldo while teaching him to restrain himself from aggression during such interactions. In the first two weeks, time-out produced the desired change. In that period, Darrian required only four time-outs. Additionally, he also learned how to behave once he was placed in time-out. Given the success achieved in the home environment, we then focused on his problems at school.

At school, he was also aggressive to classmates. We agreed that time-out would probably work at school as well. Felicia went to the teacher to request their use of time-out for this problem. Upon hearing that she was being asked to use time-out with Darrian, the teacher remarked to Felicia, "Dr. Cipani's recommendation goes against everything I was taught at the junior college about child behavior. Time-out is an abusive and ineffective strategy to deal with child problems, let alone Darrian's problems. Don't you think that we know more than Dr. Cipani about Darrian's needs? Time-out is inhumane." (*Note to reader: Apparently kicking him out of preschool is the more humane approach!*)

Once Felicia convinced the teacher to go along with the time-out, pointing to its success in the home, I met with the teacher. She agreed to use it in school for Darrian's aggressive behavior. Within a few applications of time-out, its effect at school was pronounced. The teacher was elated with

Darrian's progress. In one of my last follow-up visits to the preschool program, the teacher made the following remark, " You know, you should go to the junior college and teach them how to use time-out." She went from being a great detractor of time-out to championing its cause across the land.

At home, with aggressive behavior at a very low level, we targeted another major problem area. Darrian, like many young children, presented difficulty in getting ready for school in the morning. The plan designed made Darrian's access to TV in the morning a function of his being ready for school. Once Darrian was dressed, groomed, and ate breakfast, he then watched TV until it was time to get in the car. If he did not get ready on time, he lost morning TV. Within the first two weeks, Felicia reported that there was no longer a problem getting Darrian ready for school on time.

Another problem area was bedtime. Darrian like many other 4-year-old children, hated to go to bed. He tried everything to postpone bedtime. The $10,000 question is: "What consequence can be used to have Darrian get to bed on time?" The answer came in the form of a tradition in many households, the bedtime story. Felicia or Rinaldo read Darrian a bedtime story each night. What if a bedtime story was provided only if Darrian earned it? If Darrian was in bed by a certain time, he was read a story. However, if he was not, then it was end of story, lights out. He must have liked his stories because this problem area changed for the better within a short period of time with this contingency.

Darrian's compliance to simple directives was also addressed. Rinaldo and Felicia were taught how to be more effective in compliance situations (Cipani, 1999). I also introduced a structured game to improve Darrian's compliance, called, "The Get Me Game." This game involves the parent developing compliance by repeatedly reinforcing instruction following behavior in a short period of time (go to www.geocities.com/voivod00 for more information on this game).

The intervention effort over a 3 month period, targeted many behaviors, systematically, with success. I administered a behavioral assessment instrument, the Conner's Parent Rating Scale (CPRS) at two points during my involvement. I administered the CPRS prior to any behavioral plan being implemented (called the baseline assessment). I then administered the same CPRS three months after baseline. The change from baseline to the 3-month assessment is depicted below for 3 categories of the CPRS. The scores are reported as standard scores.

Conner's Score	baseline	3 months
Learning problems	65*	58
Impulsive-hyperactive	65*	58
Hyperactivity index	67*	57

*clinically significant above the norm

Darrian's score in each of the three categories dropped to within normal limits over the course of the intervention effort. It was evident to all who were in daily contact with Darrian that he had changed for the better.

Rome was not built in a day. Darrian took 3 months.

References

Alexander, R. N., Corbett, T. F., & Smigel, J. (1976). The effects of individual and group consequences on school attendance and curfew violations with predelinquent adolescents. *Journal of Applied Behavior Analysis, 9,* 221-226.

Aman, M. G., & Singh, N. (1979). The usefulness of thioridazine in childhood disorders: Fact or folklore? *American Journal of Mental Deficiency, 84,* 331-338.

Azrin, N. H. (1970). Punishment of elicited aggression. *Journal of the Experimental Analysis of Behavior, 14,* 7-10.

Azrin, N. H. (1960). Effects of punishment intensity during variable interval reinforcement. *Journal of the Experimental Analysis of Behavior, 3,* 123-142.

Azrin, N. H., Hake, D. F., Holz, D. F., & Hutchinson, R. R. (1965). Motivational aspects of escape from punishment. *Journal of the Experimental Analysis of Behavior, 8,* 31-44.

Azrin, N. H., & Holz, W. C. (1966). Punishment. In W. K. Honig (Ed.), *Operant behavior: Areas of research and application.* New York, NY: Appleton-Century-Crofts.

Azrin, N. H., Holz, W. C., & Hake, D. (1963). Fixed-ratio punishment. *Journal of the Experimental Analysis of Behavior, 6,* 141-148.

Azrin, N. H., Hutchinson, R. R., & Hake, D. F. (1966). Extinction-induced aggression. *Journal of the Experimental Analysis of Behavior, 9,* 191-204.

Azrin, N. H., Hutchinson, R. R., & Hake, D. F. (1967). Attack, avoidance, and escape reactions to aversive shock. *Journal of the Experimental Analysis of Behavior, 10,* 131-148.

Azrin, N. H., & Powers, M. A. (1975). Eliminating classroom disturbance of emotionally disturbed children by positive practice procedures. *Behavior Therapy, 6,* 525-534.

Bailey, J. S., Wolf, M. M., & Phillips, E. L. (1970). Home-based reinforcement and the medication of pre-delinquents' classroom behavior. *Journal of Applied Behavior Analysis, 3,* 223-233.

Barnard, J. D., Christopherson, E. R., & Wolf, M. M. (1977). Teaching children appropriate shopping behavior through parent training in the supermarket setting. *Journal of Applied Behavior Analysis, 10,* 49-60.

Bean, A. W., & Roberts, M. W. (1981). The effect of time-out release contingencies on changes in child noncompliance. *Journal of Abnormal Child Psychology, 9,* 95-105.

Bettleheim, B. (1967). *The empty fortress.* New York: Free Press.

Bornstein, P. H., Hamilton, S. B., & Quevillon, R. P. (1977). Behavior modification by long-distance: Demonstration of functional control over disruptive behavior in a rural classroom setting. *Behavior Modification, 1,* 369-380.

California Education Code of Regulations. (1993, May). *Positive Behavioral Intervention Regulations* (Section 3001 and 3052, Title 5). California.

Cipani, E. (1999). *Helping parents help their kids: A clinical guide to six child problem behaviors.* Philadelphia, PA: Bruner-Mazel.

Cipani, E. (2004). *Classroom management for all teachers; 12 plans for evidence-based practice.* Saddle River, N.J.: Prentice Hall.

Cipani, E., Brendlinger, J., McDowell, L. & Usher, S. (1991). Continuous vs. intermittet punishment: A case study. *Journal of Developmental and Physical Disabilities, 3,* 147-156.

Clark, H. B., Greene, B. F., Macrae, J. W., McNees, M. P., Davis, J. C., & Risley, T. R. (1977). A parent advice package for family shopping trips: Development and evaluation. *Journal of Applied Behavior Analysis, 10,* 604-624.

Clark, H. B., Rowbury, T., Baer, A. M., & Baer, D. M. (1973). Timeout as a punishing stimulus in continuous and intermittent schedules. *Journal of Applied Behavior Analysis, 6,* 443-456.

Dinsmoor, J. A. (1998). Punishment. In W. O'Donohue (Ed.), *Learning and behavior therapy* (pp. 188-204). Boston, MA: Allyn & Bacon.

Dreikurs, R. & Grey, L. (1968). *A new approach to discipline: Logical consequences.* New York: Hawthorne Books.

Estes, W. K. (1944). An experimental study of punishment. *Psychological Monographs, 57,* 263.

Fantino, E. J. & Logan, L. A. (1979). *The experimental analysis of behavior: A biological perspective.* (pg. 261). San Francisco: Freeman Publishers.

Goleman, D. (1995). *Emotional intelligence.* New York: Bantam Books.

Greene, B. F., Bailey, J. S., & Barber, F. (1981). An analysis and reduction of disruptive behavior on school bus. *Journal of Applied Behavior Analysis, 14,* 177-192.

Grusec, J. E., & Walters, G. C. (1977). *Punishment.* San Francisco: Freeman Publishers.

Holz, W. C. & Azrin, N. H. (1963). A comparison of several procedures for eliminating behavior. *Journal of the Experimental Analysis of Behavior, 6,* 399-406.

Iwata, B. A., & Bailey, J. S. (1974). Reward versus cost token systems: An analysis of the effects on students and teacher. *Journal of Applied Behavior Analysis, 7,* 567-576.

Lau, W., & Cipani, E. (1984). Reducing student food waste in a cafeteria-style dining room through contingency management. *Child Care Quarterly, 12,* 301-308.

Lerman, D. C., & Vorndran, C. M. (2002). On the status of knowledge for using punishment: Implications for treating behavior disorders. *Journal of Applied Behavior Analysis, 35,* 431-464.

Lovaas, O. I., & Simmons, J. Q. (1969). Manipulation of self-destruction in three retarded children. *Journal of Applied Behavior Analysis, 2,* 143-157.

Matson, J. L. & DiLorenzo, T. J. (1984). *Punishment and its alternatives: A new perspective for behavior modification.* New York: Springer Publisher Co.

Matthews, J. R., Friman, P.C., Barunc, V. J., Ross, L. V., & Christophersen, E. R. (1987). Decreasing dangerous infant behaviors through parent instruction. *Journal of Applied Behavior Analysis, 20,* 165-169.

O'Brien, F. (1989). Punishment for people with developmental disabilities. In E. Cipani (Ed.), *Treating severe behavior disorders: Behavior analysis approaches* (pp. 37-58). Washington, DC: American Association on Mental Retardation.

Otto, R. G. (1976, April). *A comparison of positive reinforcement and punishment in two special education classes.* Paper presented at the Council for Exceptional Children Convention, Chicago, IL.

Perone, M. (2003). Negative effects of positive reinforcement. *The Behavior Analyst, 26,* 1-14.

Pfiffner, L. J., & O'Leary, S. G. (1987). The efficacy of all-positive management as a function of the prior use of negative consequences. *Journal of Applied Behavior Analysis, 20,* 265-271.

Roberts, M. W., & Powers, S. W. (1990). Adjusting chair timeout enforcement procedures for oppositional children. *Behavior Therapy, 21,* 257-271.

Sajwaj, T., Libet, J., & Agras, S. (1974). Lemon-juice therapy: The control of life-threatening rumination in a six-month-old infant. *Journal of Applied Behavior Analysis, 7,* 557-563.

Sears, R. R., Maccoby, E. E., & Levin, H. (1957). *Patterns of child rearing.* Evanston, IL: Row, Peterson Publishing.

Shafto, F., & Sulzbacher, S. (1977). Comparing treatment tactics with a hyperactive preschool child: Stimulant medication and programmed teacher interventions. *Journal of Applied Behavior Analysis, 10,* 13-20.

Skinner, B. F. (1938). *The behavior of organisms: An experimental analysis.* Acton, Ma.: Copley.

Solnick, J. V., Rincover, A., & Peterson, C. R. (1977). Some determinants of the reinforcing and punishing effects of time out. *Journal of Applied Behavior Analysis, 10,* 415-424.

Straus, M. A. (1994). *Beating the devil out of them: Corporal punishment in american families.* New York: Lexington Books.

Switzer, E. B., Deal, T. E., & Bailey, J. S. (1977). The reduction of stealing in second graders using a group contingency. *Journal of Applied Behavior Analysis, 10,* 267-272.

Ulrich, R. E., & Azrin, N. H. (1962). Reflexive fighting in response to aversive structure. *Journal of the Experimental Analysis of Behavior, 5,* 511-520.

White, A. G., & Bailey, J. S. (1990). Reducing disruptive behaviors of elementary physical education students with sit and watch. *Journal of Applied Behavior Analysis, 23,* 353-359.

Zeilberger, J., Sampen, S. E., & Sloane, H. W. Jr. (1968). Modification of a child's problem behaviors in the home with the mother as therapist. *Journal of Applied Behavior Analysis, 1,* 47-54.